Why Just Surv … To THRIVE

THRIVE

5 Keys Steps to Living a Pain and Stress-Free Life

Dr Jason Gould DC

To access the range of free resources which accompany this book, including videos, worksheets and exercises, please visit **www.5tothrive.co.uk**

Author: Jason Gould : THRIVE

ISBN: 978-1-9163736-0-0

Category: Healing, Chiropractic & Mental health

Contents

Disclaimer

This book and the 5 to Thrive Health® System are focused on providing guidance on stress management, healthy habits and general well-being that can enable you to improve your health and live a thriving life. They are based on the author's over 15 years' experience as a chiropractor and health and well-being mentor.

Each person is a unique individual with his/her unique history, routine, body and mind. Any expected result mentioned in the book or in the 5 to Thrive Health® System may vary from one person to the other. Besides, the results will also vary depending on your actions and omissions in the development of healthy habits.

Therefore, the author does not guarantee any expected results mentioned in the book or in the 5 to Thrive Health® System and will not be liable if for any reason you cannot achieve results similar to the expected results mentioned in the book or in the 5 to Thrive Health® System.

The author is not a doctor, nutritionist, psychologist, psychiatrist or counsellor.

Therefore, nothing in this book or in the 5 to Thrive Health® System will or will be deemed to:

- give medical, nutritional, psychological or psychiatric advice,
- provide diagnosis,
- prescribe treatments,
- prescribe medication,
- give advice on physiotherapy.

Always consult a doctor, nutritionist, psychologist, psychiatrist and/or counsellor, if you experience any physical or mental discomfort, difficulty or pain, before you take any medication or start any treatment and/or if you have any concerns about your health.

The author is not and will not be deemed to be liable for:

- your health and safety,
- your acts or omissions in developing your life habits,
- whether or not you consult a doctor, nutritionist, psychologist, psychiatrist and/or counsellor when necessary.

Acknowledgements

There are so many people to thank who have contributed significantly to help me develop the skills, tools and expertise that have led to the creation of this book.

I would firstly like to thank Tara, my incredibly loving and patient wife who has been there through the challenges that helped me and inspired me to grow and bring our vision to the world. You have been extremely supportive and made many personal sacrifices to support our mission.

Jo and Steve Davison – Steve your 'What's the Story Morning Glory' was the catalyst that actually started this project.

Dr Heidi Haavik for your persistent hard work and research into our amazing Chiropractic profession and your permission to reference your work here – thank you.

Dr Dennis Perman and Dr Bob Hoffman of the Masters Circle for your mentorship over the years.

Dr Russ Rosen for your help and support and permission to develop your work '3 Dimensions of Stress'.

Thank you to my wonderful and dedicated team at Chislehurst Chiropractic Clinic for your help and support and the fantastic care that you give our patients.

A special thank you to Becki Davey – without your persistent help and support this book would not have made its completion deadline.

Also, and in no particular order for help, inspiration, input and support I acknowledge and thank Dr Fab Mancini, Dr John Demartini, Dr Ross McDonald, Dr Paul McCrossin, Dr James Chestnut, Dr Niels Peter Carstens, Dr Meena Kharade, Dr Misty Thorn, Mr Bobby Siddiqui, Peter Godfrey, Anthony Robbins, Gianfranco Zola, Michelle Watson, Jackie Barrie, Andy Harrington, Melissa Sandford, Gemma Le-Page, Kelly Jarvis and Jessen James.

And lastly, but most definitely not least, thank you to Emma Byrne, your friendship and ongoing support means so much.

I would like to dedicate this book to my incredible children, I love you both to the universe and back.

In loving memory of my Grandma – you have left a legacy of love and kindness that lives on through your children, grandchildren and great-grandchildren.

Readers' Comments for 'Thrive'

Every sportsperson needs their body to perform at its optimal potential and just as importantly, their mindset needs to be strong and focused. 'Thrive' has a wealth of knowledge and practical advice for those looking to get their body and mind performing at their best.

- Gianfranco Zola, MBE and OMRI
Football Manager and Former Professional Footballer

• • •

'Thrive' is a powerful and practical book that will inspire you on your journey to living a life full of vibrant health and inner well-being.

- Dr John Demartini
International Best-Selling Author of The Values Factor

• • •

Jason Gould's 'Thrive' is an accessible and engaging look into how the stresses we encounter everyday can negatively affect our health. He will give you an insight into how choices, changes and chiropractic care can vastly improve your health and vitality. This is a must read!

- Dr Fabrizio Mancini
International Best-Selling Author, Speaker and Media Healthy Living Expert

I have known Dr Jason for many years. He is passionate about helping his patients and community be the best version of themselves by empowering them to THRIVE! By delivering these simple nuggets of health wisdom, Dr Jason encourages his readers to take action and to move from surviving to thriving, improving their own life and that of their friends and family. It is a must read for anyone who has ever questioned about gaining better health or is fed up of being sick and fed up!

- *Ross McDonald, DC*
President of the Scottish Chiropractic Association

• • •

Jason is an extremely passionate and knowledgeable human being. His information is digestible and relevant. He is inspiring not only to his colleagues but also the wider community in which he serves. Get this book on your 'must read' list.

- *Melissa Sandford*
CEO, United Chiropractic Association

• • •

I have watched Dr Jason Gould's evolution, from enthusiastic student to gifted healer to persuasive presenter and now, with 'Thrive' he emerges as a significant thought leader. This entertaining and thought-provoking book provides essential insights into health and wellness, offering a model for optimizing lifestyle that anyone can operate and everyone will benefit from. In a clogged and crowded marketplace on this topic, 'Thrive' has something fresh and important to say.

- *Dr Dennis Perman*
Co-Founder of The Masters Circle Global

'Thrive' should be the first port of call for everybody on a journey to better health. It takes a multifaceted approach, which highlights the specific factors that are stopping you thriving and is a complete guide to what you can do TODAY to start and succeed on your journey to optimal health and wellness. A great read from an exceptional chiropractor and health professional.

- ***Russ Rosen***
Health and Wellness Mentor and Pioneer

• • •

A must read for seekers of optimal health and well-being!

- ***Steve Davidson***
Co-creator of Blue Cow Practice and Blue Cow Business

• • •

If health and well-being are important to you, this book by Dr Jason Gould has to be the one and only lifestyle book you will ever need. This manual for life covers every aspect of well-being, focusing on 7 essential elements vital to living a happy and healthy life. As a GP of 25 years' experience, this is the book I would like all my patients to read.

- ***Dr Meena Kharade***
GP

As modern medicine has shifted towards a more holistic approach, patient-centred care and patient empowerment is key to this ideal.

Many medical and surgical conditions can have their development slowed down and even reversed by adopting a healthy body, mind and lifestyle.

'Thrive' addresses this head on by providing the reader with the knowledge, skills and strategies necessary for tackling a modern-day lifestyle to improve overall well-being.

By recognising the main sources of stress (and thereby avoiding them) and through mastery of one's own mind, Dr Gould puts the patient in the driving seat of their own health journey.

As an orthopaedic surgeon, I highly recommend this book to patients and the well alike. I strongly believe that reader empowerment can influence their overall health and 'Thrive' remains vital to enable the reader to 'heal thyself'.

- *Mr. Bobby Siddiqui*
Orthopaedic Surgeon

• • •

In a world where an underlying level of stress has become 'normal', Jason's book nudges you back to physical and mental health (much like a chiropractic adjustment).

It includes medical information made simple, diagnostic questionnaires, helpful acronyms, and a wealth of practical advice presented in an accessible, clear and logical way.

When you want to take your health seriously, the best thing you can do is buy it, read it, and act on the advice within.

- *Jackie Barrie*
Trainer, Speaker, Copywriter, Author

I have worked with Jason on the '5 to Thrive Health®' programme for a year and will continue working with Jason on a maintenance programme. When I first started working with Jason, I was diagnosed with Lyme disease, Chronic Fatigue Syndrome and Fibromyalgia and my health had taken a real dramatic decline. I had to take six months off work and stop all activity. Since working with Jason over the last year, my health has drastically improved and I am now back to work part-time. Jason has really helped me in many ways not just with chiropractic care. Jason helped build my confidence back up in my body again. Jason has helped me regain my health in a holistic way looking at all areas that contribute to good health. I am so thankful for Jason, his ongoing support and help throughout my recovery journey.

- *Kelly Jarvis*
'5 to Thrive Health®' System Client

• • •

Praise to Jason for 'Thrive', this book we should all being applying to our lives.

Having been lucky enough to work with Jason, I know these methods work, you just need to take the steps and results speak for themselves.

'Thrive' is not only about a diet but also a lifestyle. We are not only what we eat but how we live. This is becoming a problem in today's fast-paced environment, affecting our everyday life. Jason outlines this and helps us identify these issues; he gives us insights and advice on how we can deal with them and get balance to our whole life. Therefore, we can thrive.

Jason is very committed to his patients. His drive to help people not only shines through this book but also through his clinic and staff.

- *Gemma Le-Page*
5 to Thrive Health® Svstem Client

Jason Gould is a phenomenal man, why? When I met Jason, I was struggling with pain. I had a lot of pain in my lower back, I had pain shooting down my legs and to be quite honest, it was affecting me mentally, physically and emotionally. I could not even get up out of bed in the morning. This meant I couldn't interact with my children, I couldn't get to work, I couldn't even run my business properly, all of these areas of my life started getting impacted. I went and met Jason and started working with him. I received chiropractic care and one-to-one health coaching from him.

If you are someone right now that wants to fire on all cylinders, if you want to optimise your performance, or perhaps you're in physical and mental pain right now and it's affecting how you make your money, maybe affecting how you get your work done. Then I would highly recommend you listen to your body and get in touch with Jason Gould. He will help you.

What he's done for me is reverse something that doctors said I needed surgery for. I had a bulging lower disc and I was told I needed to have surgery. However, from chiropractic care, health coaching and adjustments to my diet, I was able to take that and reverse it. As a result of that, my business has flown, my relationships have gotten stronger, my health is better than it's ever been.

I'm telling you right now, if you are a business owner, or you're in employment right now and you're looking to really excel in your career, your health is the number one thing that is going to take you there. So, do yourself a favour, read 'Thrive' and book yourself in with Jason. Get in touch with him, if you get the opportunity to meet him or work with him in any capacity, grab it with both hands, your future self will thank you for it.

- ***Jessen James***

Serial Entrepreneur, Business Mentor and Multi-Award-Winning International Speaker

Foreword

You do not need to THRIVE to begin, you need to begin [to read this book] to THRIVE. It's time to take control of your destiny.

A foreword by Peter Godfrey, Chairman of a number of companies, FIRST A Global Agency, TXG, Chill Chain, iRecycle, former President of American Express Global Network Services, member of the directors' board for Brighton and Hove Albion football club and sport and health enthusiast. Chairman of Chris Aked Cancer Foundation.

I was recommended by a number of friends to see Jason Gould as I had multiple injuries which had occurred from decades of playing sport. Some two years later, not only do I continue to seek Jason's professional chiropractic help for my body, but we have become good friends and have been able to exchange our knowledge and wisdom on many fronts.

I was delighted when I was approached to write a foreword for this compelling book, 'Thrive'. On one of my many visits to Jason, we discussed his desire to write a captivating book on the many aspects that make up this complex mind and body of ours. Interestingly at the time, I discovered that linked to his thinking, the notion of 'The Dash' was very much in the front of my mind. In essence, we are born with on average 42,000,000 million minutes for men and 43,500,000 for women (that's for the acute minded), around 79/80 years for men and 82/83 years for women. I called that universally our 'dash', so as the famous strap line says, 'life is too good to waste'. My foreword is the maximisation of your life or dash.

When thinking about 'thriving' in life and the sequence of events, circumstances, and happenings attributed to the adjective, it's important to ask yourself why; why do you want to thrive? I think of it as the creation and shaping of 'The Dash'. 'The Dash' is located on a gravestone between the date of birth and the date of death but is more than just a marking, it symbolises one's life moments and achievements, no matter the period of time it represents. Whilst seemingly inconsequential, that little dash can represent a life well spent.

Linking and marrying passion and knowledge, Jason has crafted this book highlighting a fundamental checklist to help you stop just surviving and start thriving, to create your dash – that powerful little line that narrates 'I lived here, and I achieved this'. When magnified and examined in closer detail, the dash is a collection or series of parts forming one's life. Each fragment is representative of all of the aspects that make up our life, and therefore, it's up to us to determine the formation of our dash. There will always be external factors out of our control, but we must forget the notion of being reactive and begin focusing on being pre- and pro-active. As you read this book, you will be familiarised with the seven essential elements to create optimum health, clearly detailed and supported by theory. From there, it's up to you to take control of the scribe, no one else is here to do it for you. After all, we came to this world with nothing and we will leave this world with nothing, but it's what we do in between that matters; it's the dash that matters.

It's all too common for us as individuals to become complacent, to address issues as they arise and to do the bare minimum just to survive. But why just survive when you can thrive? It's profound how understanding the link between the 5 Dimensions of Stress and your mental and physical health can be obtained by reading this book. Why wait for curve balls to be thrown your way to trigger change when you can pre-actively learn of the fundamentals of good health, and pro-actively prevent poor well-being and no quality of life. With the information and tools Jason has detailed within, you have the ability to do better. You're in control of your mind and your body and therefore you have significant control over your 'dash'. You have a choice in life to either passively let life take its course or actively research, plan, question and single-mindedly decide to steer your own path as much as one can.

This book allows you to decide your destiny, learn to adopt and adapt based on what's been demonstrated by the very knowledgeable and truly passionate Jason Gould and you will be equipped to THRIVE! It would be remiss of me to even suggest that you 'read a book and, Bobs your uncle' and/or we think we have cracked the code... 'hallelujah'. The book is more there to help steer and navigate your own destiny and enables one to consider that good or great input and wisdom could be the difference in the quality and length of your personal dash.

You do not need to THRIVE to begin, you need to begin [to read this book] to THRIVE.

- Peter Godfrey, Older ------ Preneur

Preface

This book is based on 7 essential elements to create optimum health:

Health Principle 1
Your body is incredible - it is self-healing and self-regulating.

Health Principle 2
Your nervous system is your master system. It controls every cell, every tissue and every organ in your body.

Health Principle 3
The food we eat is the greatest form of medicine or the slowest form of poison.

Health Principle 4
Your posture is the window to your spine.

Health Principle 5
Movement creates energy – energy creates life.

Health Principle 6
There are 5 Dimensions of Stress. When your body can no longer adapt you start to go into a state of dis-ease and this can eventually lead to you becoming injured or sick or lead to a state of disease.

Health Principle 7
Your environment can affect your gene expression.

Why Just Survive When You Were Born To THRIVE?

INTRODUCTION

What does health mean to you?

So many people could feel better, every day, yet they don't necessarily know how or where to start. Not knowing about how to improve your health can lead to unnecessary suffering, affecting your overall well-being and quality of life. With the stresses and strains of daily life, many people exist in survival mode. They are on autopilot, getting through each day with low energy levels, experiencing trouble with their memory and feeling exhausted by the time their head hits the pillow for another restless night's sleep. If they feel pain, they take painkillers and trudge on.

Despite advances in health care, we seem to be seeing more serious health problems in younger people. We are now at an ever-increasing risk that, for the first time in history, our children will have a shorter lifespan than us. As I am writing this book there are news reports of pilots crashing planes due to mental health problems. Stress, overwhelm, pain and suffering tragically affect millions of lives. Yet despite all these challenges there are some people who really are thriving. These are people who have experienced debilitating adversity and have managed to come back from it, turn things around and THRIVE.

For most people, health is more than just being pain-free. It's about living a vibrant, healthy lifestyle. The intention of this book is to help you understand your own health and to empower you to live your life to the fullest.

You do not need to go into crisis mode before you begin to work on your health. We all know that 'prevention is better than cure'.

The great news is that you also have the capacity to start every day feeling energetic and happy, with strong physical health and a positive mental and emotional state. You can perform at your peak, reduce your chances of suffering from strains, illness and disease, improve your ability to cope with stress and rediscover your zest for life. Drawing on my professional and personal experience, this book offers you key actionable steps to regain control of your health. Rather than living in 'fight-or-flight' survival mode, you can learn to THRIVE.

What is thriving? Well, it's being vibrant, energetic and facing life head on. It's having the ability to be in the eye of the storm, with all the complications life brings swirling around you and staying centred and calm. Thriving is being able to work well under pressure, after a great night's sleep and with peak physical health. It's having a zest for life and loving what you do. From my experience, it's fundamentally about having a great quality of life, but also a great expression of health. It's more than just fitness and being able to do what you want. This isn't a selfish want: remember, your health affects everything you do and everyone you know. If you're healthy you'll be a better companion and partner, as well as being able to perform better in your professional life.

You've picked up this book because you're interested in your health and in taking steps to improve it. Maybe you have low back pain with a constant deep, gnawing, tooth-achy pain, with intermittent sharp twinges or stabbing pain, that is affecting sleep, or your ability to put your shoes and socks on, or get up and down from a chair and it's affecting your overall quality of life.

Or perhaps your energy is not quite what it should be and you find yourself reaching for the snooze button, craving sugary snacks and caffeine. Maybe you suffer from that mid-afternoon slump which means that you feel like your brain is in a fog and you can't quite remember what you need to and you are fed up with feeling run down and fatigued.

Possibly, you know you are not eating the right foods; you have maybe even tried diets that haven't worked or struggle to get into healthy habits. Exercise programmes have failed and you have clothes in the wardrobe that no longer fit.

Maybe you get stressed, frustrated and find that it's hard to sleep, or that you are suffering with headaches or anxiety and are keen to stay off prescription medication.

Potentially you already see yourself as healthy in some areas, yet you know there are other areas you would love to improve upon and really invest in your long-term health.

Well, imagine you've got that spring in your step, that vibrancy, that energy. You don't have to worry about re-injuring yourself because you have that confidence back in your body and you have a new love for healthy, mouth-watering and nutritious foods. Your mind is clear and focused and your memory is great. You have created an inspiring lifestyle. You know exactly what exercise you love to do; you want to understand the foods that you are eating, what foods create energy and what foods take it away. You have strategies and resources in place to cope with stress. You have the ability to really understand your body better than ever before and your health is improving every day.

You might be wondering, okay, how can I get from being in pain, or being exhausted or fatigued, to a place of energy, passion and vibrancy? As a chiropractor, that's exactly what I help people to do every day. There is so much more to health than being pain-free. The body also has an incredible power to heal itself (which we will explore in more detail later). My mission is to give people the tools for long lasting health so that they can really THRIVE, tools that I've developed through my personal and professional experience. I'm going to share those tools with you in this book and let you know where you can go from here if you really want to have lasting change in the new lifestyle that you aspire to.

I've taken the steps that I'm going to share with you in this book in my own life. Have you ever had a time in your life where you knew that you have needed to make a change and been told to think outside the box?

So, come with me to the beginning of my story. It's November 1990. I am twelve years old and we're standing near my desk in my first-year school classroom. You will see a room full of wooden desks and smell the stale aroma of sweaty gym kits, well it is an all-boys school after all. Everyone is starting to come back in from break.

Suddenly, there's a vice like grip on my arm and as I turn, I see the school bully. He mutters something under his breath but I don't hear a word. All I can focus on is the icy sensation of the knife he has placed under my throat.

I feel panic rip through me and yet with it, a rush of adrenaline that brings a strange relief. I am lucky to walk away with a hard beating but it could have been so much worse.

Something changed in me after that day. For the first time in six years, I decided enough was enough. It was time to make a change. Time to develop courage in the face of adversity.

I made a decision to become stronger. I learned judo and started playing rugby for the school team. I found myself for the first time in my life being strong enough physically and emotionally to stand up for myself. Although the bullying stopped, the stress from those early years had a negative impact on my health, which I didn't realise until much later.

Let's move forward to October 1994. You are with me in my family lounge, standing there with my dad, an older, greyer, wrinkly version of me and I'm anxiously waiting to receive some news.

"Jason, I just got off the phone with the doctor and your blood test shows that you've got glandular fever, you can't go to Kelly College."

"Dad, what do you mean, I'm going, the bus is waiting, my bags are packed. If you don't take me, I'll walk there myself."

"Jason, you can't go. You've got glandular fever. If you go, you will make yourself really sick. It's a leadership course, you'll be sleeping outside in tents. Also, your spleen is enlarged you will need to make other changes as well. No more rugby or judo, I'm sorry, Jason."

"But dad, you don't understand, I have to go. Whatever it takes, I'm going."

"Jason, you're not going. That's the end of it."

You can probably imagine that Kevin and Perry scene playing out in my house. My sport was so important to me. It had given me confidence in my body and helped me to overcome the bullying I'd experienced since I was six years old. I couldn't play the sports that I loved and had lost the identity and strength I gained from doing them.

Life after that felt hard. I felt a constant and debilitating fatigue, waking up with no energy in my body and a cloud of brain fog. I had to learn to pace myself and work out what foods helped me to feel better. People didn't seem to understand and I frequently was asked, with just a hint of cynicism, "are you not better yet?" I felt awful and friends didn't seem to believe me.

I wasn't sure exactly of what to do with my life but I studied hard and started to think about a career. I wanted to do something in which I could really help people. My interest in health had spiked so I went on a search to find out more about health and maybe potentially study medicine. However, something didn't quite sit right.

I did my research and secured myself some work experience in various hospitals to get an insight into the world of medicine. It soon became apparent, after speaking to the junior doctors, that they just weren't happy in their roles, in fact, they seemed thoroughly disillusioned. "Are you sure you really want a career in medicine?" seemed to be the resounding question I was asked.

It's two years later. I am now observing a neurologist in Poole Hospital, a pivotal moment for me. A distinctive man, immaculately dressed, with swept back silver hair and wire rimmed glasses.

"We have a patient in bed three with respiratory distress. Six months ago, I could've given him the drugs that would have helped with his symptoms but red tape has stopped that. It's not life threatening, but he's going to have to suffer unnecessarily for three hours until the respiratory consultant is free to prescribe it."

It was clear to me at that point that the doctors were caring, hard-working people who wanted to do the best for their patients. Unfortunately, their 'hands were tied' where bureaucracy and budgets got in the way of patient welfare.

That was a defining moment, to continue on a career path that felt wrong for me or make a change. My dad suggested I visit a family friend, George. He was in his mid-sixties and one of those people with a glint in their eye and a true passion for what they do.

"So, Jason," he said. "I understand that you were considering medicine but now you're thinking that might not be for you? Do you know what I love about working with patients? It's the natural drug-free approach and the really incredible thing is that the body has an amazing capacity to heal and repair itself and you can help to facilitate that process by understanding what the underlying cause of the problem is. Jason, the key to your health is inside you."

It was at that moment that the pieces of the puzzle fell into place and I decided I wanted to do what George did. George was a chiropractor and that's exactly what I was going to be.

So, after completing my Pharmacology degree at Kings College London in 2001, I went to the Anglo European College of Chiropractic where I went straight into the second year of the Chiropractic degree and spent a further four years learning and training.

Let's move on once more, to me enjoying a break from studying. I'm on Bournemouth beach holding a rugby ball. It's 11 degrees Celsius and the heart of the Bournemouth summer.

I hear a shout behind me and the next thing I know, my head's spinning, there's blood pouring down my face and I'm in agony. Not my finest sporting moment! I've done a judo rolling breakfall and kneed myself in the face! Off to the clinic I go and in the next few weeks, suffering with severe headaches, I am referred for an MRI. I'm lying there thinking, "what's happened? What's going on?" My mind suddenly goes blank and I'm back feeling the physical stress of being bullied and being ill. I feel helpless until I remember George's words. "Jason, the key to your health is inside you."

I never wanted to feel like that again so I make a conscious decision to work on my health. It really works for me and a few years into my chiropractic training I am doing well; everything is going brilliantly. Then I receive a phone call from my best friend's younger brother.

I find out that one of my closest friends, at the age of 25, has died from a stroke caused by a blood clot, this was most likely a side effect of the prescription drugs that she has been on. Through one of the worst moments in my life, I realised then that I had made the right choice, I wanted to do everything I could to help people to heal naturally, without being reliant on medication.

After graduating from chiropractic college, my next big decision is to embark on setting up my own clinic. So now you can find me in a room so small that I can spread my arms and touch each wall. I literally have to move the adjusting bench and put the headpiece down just to open the door to let patients into the room. It is cosy to say the least.

I work hard and my clinic starts to grow. I decide to expand.

However, all wasn't perfect. I didn't see it creeping up on me. I found myself lying on my bench, feeling exhausted and drained. Not too dissimilar to how I felt when I had glandular fever. I was working long hours, grabbing the wrong foods when I could. I was in a carb coma and I needed to seriously think about how I was treating myself and what I was putting in my body.

So, I went back to what I knew and started exercising and eating healthily again. Everything fell into place. My body felt healthier than it had in years and I could work on my passions: for my clinic, for my patients, for karate. I became a second dan black belt and had the opportunity as a chiropractor to work with the England Goju-Ryu Karate squad at the World Championships.

I have now been fortunate enough to travel all over the world training, treating and teaching and my clinic is now a multi award-winning multidisciplinary clinic with seven treatment rooms and digital x-ray facilities. I have been awarded the International Chiropractor of the Year award, the Tony Robbins Leadership Student of the Year and received awards in professional speaking as well.

The greatest pleasure I find in my work is helping my patients to understand how they too can achieve better health. I am passionate about sharing my simple steps, so you too can learn how to THRIVE.

There's nothing special about me, what is special is the 5 Key Pillars of health that you need to THRIVE.

Rather than thinking out of the box or creating a new box sometimes you need to think inside the box, and by that, I mean the box inside you.

> The key to your health is inside you.

The key to your health is inside you and learning how to tap into it is what the 5 to THRIVE Health® System is about. What I call, the 5 Key Pillars will help you to live a life of optimal and vibrant health. This book will introduce you to the practical steps that I have developed and teach to my clients in workshops and online to enable you to begin addressing each of these points, for your journey towards optimal health.

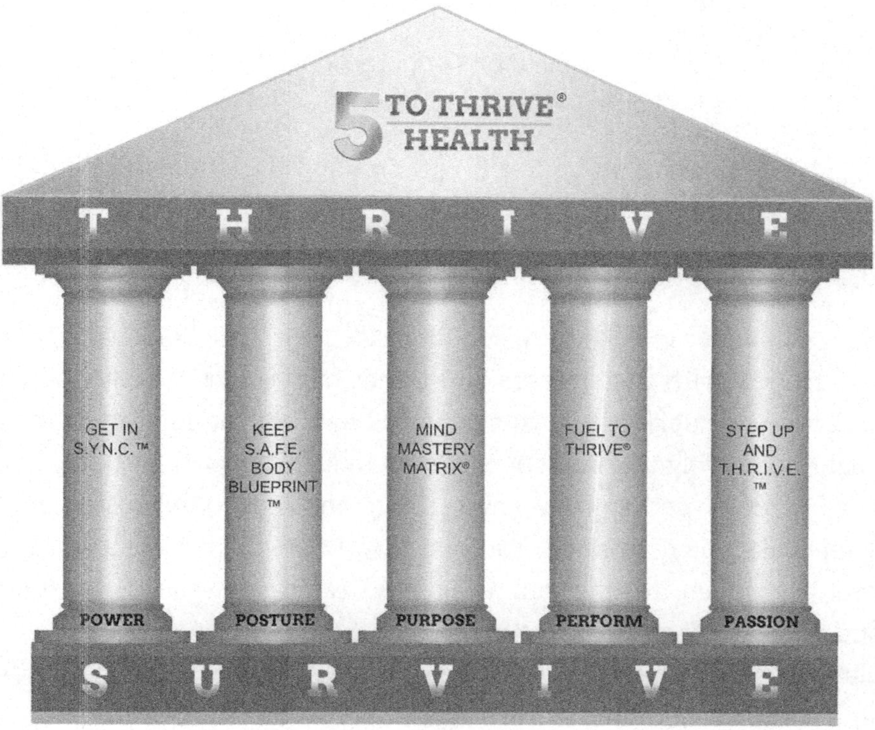

Throughout this book, you'll be encouraged to stop and reflect on your own health.

Before you begin reading, consider these questions:

1. Is your health important to you?
2. What actions and steps do you take on a daily basis to move towards health?
3. What thoughts, habits or behaviours do you have that move you away from health?
4. Other than yourself, who in your life is affected by poor quality of health?

To summarise, our journey together through this book will help you to deal with the stresses in life that damage your body and to improve your ability to maximise your health in the long-term. You might be reading this book because you have back pain, neck pain or headaches, or perhaps you have fatigue and feel so exhausted that it feels like you're in a fog. You or a loved one might have a serious health problem. Maybe you're already leading a wellness lifestyle and want to learn more. Now, imagine that you have abundant and vibrant energy, or you are living life pain-free and with a spring in your step. What would life be like? What opportunities, adventures and experiences would you be able to have if you had better health? What would your life look like today? If the idea of vibrant and optimum health interests you, read on.

Perhaps you know of an 'Uncle Joe' story? Most people know someone, or know of someone, who seemed perfectly healthy but died suddenly. Perhaps they were a fit, fifty-two-year-old father of two, who died from a massive heart attack without any warning. Although they exercised regularly, their stress levels and eating habits eventually caught up with them. Health is about more than just fitness and time is precious. It is so important to act now for your health, as your health affects everything you do and everyone you know.

> You must take personal responsibility. You cannot change the circumstances, the seasons, or the wind, but you can change yourself. That is something you have charge of.
>
> \- Jim Rohn

The 5 Dimensions of Stress

So, what affects our health and puts us into survival mode? The answer is stress, and if we look a bit deeper, there are actually different types of stress. There is physical, emotional, chemical, nutritional and environmental stress. I have called these stresses the 5 Dimensions of Stress. By understanding how these stresses affect us and where they come from, we can come up with ways to reduce, modify or eliminate them from our lives and move towards living with optimal health.

The 5 Dimensions of Stress:

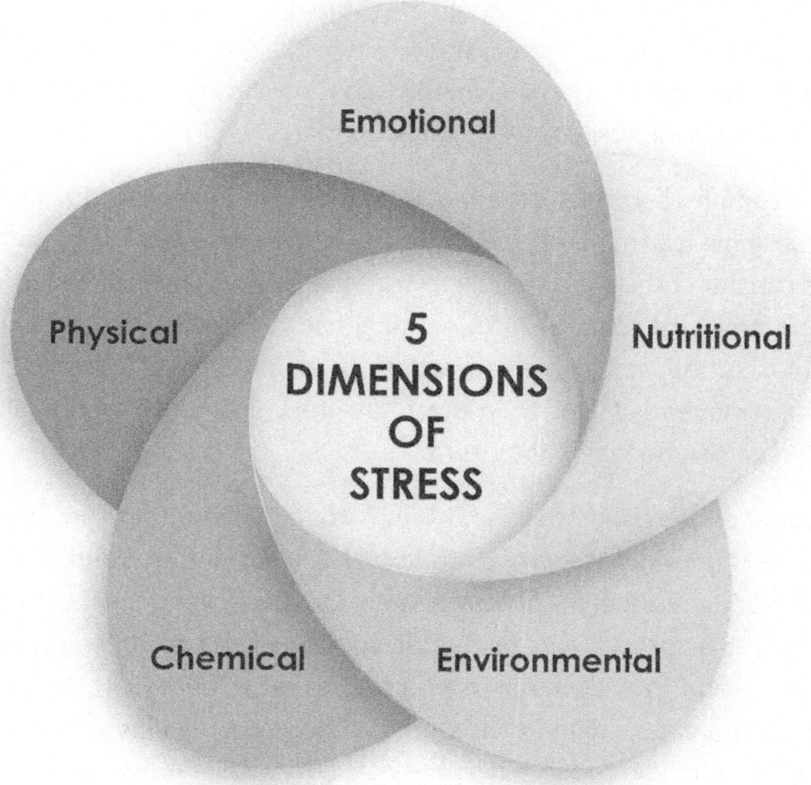

Physical Stress

So, what is physical stress and how does it affect us?

Physical stress can affect us in two ways, acute physical stress or chronic and repetitive physical stress. Acute physical stress is from a sudden event or trauma such as a car accident, a fall or even childbirth, whereas chronic physical stress could be from repetitive strains such as poor posture, lifting or even running long distances with imbalances in your joints. These day-to-day physical stresses are very common and some simple changes can really reduce their impact on you.

The injuries that people sustain can sometimes seem to 'come out of nowhere'. However, if we trace things back, there are sometimes subtle clues that can help us identify possible causes which may have been slowly and insidiously building up for a while.

For example, if you fall over you can affect the movement of bones in the spine (called vertebrae). If they become restricted in movement this can affect the small muscles either side of the spine, subsequently if this segment remains dysfunctional it can lead to imbalance and weakness that could lead to problems or injury later. This lack of proper movement can then start to affect ligaments or the discs between the vertebrae long-term.

Ligaments are straps that hold bones together and form our joints. Poor posture puts stress and strain on these ligaments and this leads to a gradual weakening. These tissues can then pull or tear which is known as a sprain. Over time your body will react to these physical stresses and can develop osteoarthritis (wear and tear), in other words, premature aging of the joints. There are specific techniques that can help you reduce this physical stress which reduces pain and speeds up recovery and, in many cases, avoids unnecessary surgery.

I have patients come into my clinic who say, “I have arthritis in my right knee, but it is to be expected because I’m getting older.” My next question to them is, “Is your right knee older than your left knee?” After they laugh about it, I often see a look of realisation on their face because both knees are obviously the same age. Osteoarthritis is actually a wear and tear process that has happened over time due to the physical stresses throughout their life. Even if you have arthritis, if you catch the joint early enough then with a combination of lifestyle advice and chiropractic treatment you can reduce the stresses on it and potentially the wear process will be less accelerated.

Prevention is obviously better than cure. So, think about what stresses you can change or modify that could be wearing you out.

The following Stress Solution Synthesiser will help you identify areas of stress in your life and if followed, will form the building blocks to help dramatically reduce these stresses. Let’s look at the First Dimension, Physical Stress.

The 5 Dimensions of Stress

Stress Solution Synthesiser

1. Physical Stress – Please tick all that apply

	Physical stress	Possible new action steps
☐	Sitting for too long	Take a break Get up and move around
☐	Standing still for too long	Take a break Sit down or walk around Change footwear
☐	Poor exercise technique	Get professional advice Change exercise
☐	Lack of exercise	Start to exercise Get advice on how to exercise safely
☐	Repetitive strains	Change posture Strengthen core Chiropractic adjustments
☐	Heavy lifting	Get help Break down into smaller objects Use a lumbar support belt Do warm up exercises
☐	Carrying a bag over the shoulder	Use a rucksack Carry less and lighten the load Swap / alternate shoulders
☐	Car accidents	Get specialist chiropractic advice for rehabilitation

☐	Slips, trips and falls	Change footwear Do balance exercises Have chiropractic adjustments
☐	Surgery	Sometimes surgery can be prevented Perform Prehab prior to surgery (Prehab is a combination of chiropractic adjustments and an exercise programme to prepare your body. Prepare a rehabilitation programme for after surgery
☐	Uncomfortable furniture (chair, sofa, bed, car seat)	Change furniture or desk Use a posture support cushion Use a standing desk
☐	Using smart devices and computers with poor posture	Check and improve your posture Reduce your time before you take a break Use dictation software or earphones / speakerphones
☐	Poor posture	Chiropractic adjustments Posture exercises Change furniture
☐	Sprains or fractures	Prevention through core stability
☐	Other	Treatment and exercise programme

When looking through the Physical Dimension of Stress, remember this is not an exhaustive list, this is to give you an idea of areas for you to focus on. A great question to ask yourself to start to make change is:

'Can I stop, modify, change, or seek advice or specialist help?'

Emotional Stress

Stress is actually defined as our body's response to the environment; however, we typically refer to a negative emotional event as the stress that has an impact on our mental and physical well-being.

So, what happens during the stress response?

Stress is the body's method of reacting to a challenge. This is controlled by the Central Nervous System which activates a fight-or-flight response (the sympathetic system) and because the body cannot keep this state for long periods of time it is designed to return it to a normal state using rest, digest and heal (the parasympathetic system). Returning the body's physiological conditions to normal is known as 'homeostasis'.

The challenge we face is that a particularly horrible event in life might cause us emotional pain, however, the continuous levels of pressure on a daily basis change the hormones circulating in our bodies. These stress hormones, adrenaline (also known as epinephrine) and cortisol, are just a couple of the hormones that get released during the stress response.

The muscles become ready to be used as the body goes into a state of red alert. Your jaw, neck and shoulder muscles become tense. The following physiological changes occur in our body due to emotional stress:

- Increased cortisol
- Increased catecholamines (including adrenaline and noradrenaline)
- Increased heart rate
- Increased vasoconstriction
- Increased blood pressure
- Increased blood glucose levels
- Increased blood lipid levels
- Increased blood cholesterol levels (increased LDL, decreased HDL)
- Increased clotting factors
- Increased protein degradation of muscle and connective-tissue
- Insulin resistance, leading to pre-diabetic stress
- Increased feelings of stress, fear, anxiety and depression
- Decreased short-term memory, ability to concentrate and learn new material
- Decreased serotonin levels; increased adrenaline levels

These responses are actually the body's natural physiological approach to help protect you. The real underlying problem is not the physiological change to stress (such as raised heart rate) rather the problem comes from the environment or thoughts we have that create the stress response in the first place. Additionally, it is the frequency and duration, or in some cases never ending levels of 'stress', that contribute to our health problems.

The long-term effects of stress ultimately lead to the body breaking down. In other words, stress leads to significantly increased risk of heart attack, stroke, diabetes, mental illness, memory loss, poor functioning immune system and ultimately, a risk of early death.

It is clear that we need stress for survival in the event of danger. For example, if a tiger jumped out at you, you would go into a state of fight-or-flight. This means that the body becomes primed to either fight or run away. In fact, the nervous system acts like the conductor of an orchestra and using the normal physiological response the body adapts by going into a survival mode.

In today's world, the demands on us have dramatically increased, where everything needs to be done NOW or even yesterday. Tony Robbins often refers to this as a 'nano-second culture'. Our general state could be described as one of constant, chronic low levels of stress. In the past, a letter would be sent to you, it would take a couple of days to arrive and you would then have time to respond. Now you receive an email in the morning and a phone call later that day, asking if you have received the email and asking why you haven't already responded. The demands on us have substantially increased.

That's the problem with modern living, we now live in habitually stressful environments. So the stress hormones remain in our bodies for far too long and cause long-term damage. Some of these physiological changes include high blood pressure, depression, impaired memory or increased resistance to glucose. As Dr James Chestnut, author of 'The Wellness & Prevention Paradigm' puts it, "as a species, humans are facing our greatest threat in history. That threat is chronic illness."[1]

Some of the larger events and stressors in life range from looking for a job, going for a promotion, moving house, death or illness of a loved one or starting a family – even exciting events cause stress. Stress can be related to your finances, work, relationships or health, just to name a few potential sources. You might have even noticed an increased heart rate or change to your breathing just in reading this paragraph.

---

1 James L. Chestnut, *The Wellness & Prevention Paradigm* (n.pl: TWP Press, 2011)

The good news is that there is so much you can do to reduce the effects of the stress response and we will discuss this in detail in the Mind Mastery Matrix® section.

Chemical Stress

Modern day life surrounds us with a multitude of chemicals which we touch, ingest and breathe in on a daily basis. These chemicals can then enter our blood stream or be stored in our fat cells. The harmful effects of these chemicals can vary from causing headaches and allergies to having a toxic effect on the brain, nervous system and body, causing long-term health problems. Here are a few common chemicals we encounter every day.

Pesticides

Modern non-organic farming techniques use high levels of pesticides to protect against tiny pests which can cause damage to crops, therefore pesticides by their nature are a poison. Pesticide residue remains on non-organically grown fruits and vegetables as well as within other processed food products. These chemicals are then ingested by you when you eat them.

Pesticides have been linked to neurological degenerative conditions. In places where pesticide accidents have occurred or where people have grown up on farms, there is an increase in conditions such as Alzheimer's Disease, Parkinson's Disease and Motor Neurone Disease.

If the option is available to you, I recommend eating organic food wherever you can. It is important to note that not all products labelled 'organic' have been grown completely without pesticides. Some chemical pesticides are allowed by law within organic farming, so do your research into the company you are buying from.

The majority of pesticide residue is found in the skin of a fruit or vegetable; however, many good nutrients are also found in the skin. One of the best options is eat organic products whole after washing them and if you are not able to purchase organic products, I recommend that you wash and peel your fruits and vegetables to remove as much of the contamination as you can.

There is a list known as 'The Clean Fifteen', which lists the fruits and vegetables which tend to have the least contamination from pesticides, these are not necessarily organic, but require less pesticides in their cultivation. It includes beetroot, mushrooms, onions, sweet potatoes and leeks, this list is paired with what is called 'The Dirty Dozen' which is a list of the twelve most contaminated fruits and vegetables, this list includes apples, parsnips, peaches and grapes.

Perfluorinated Compounds (PFCs)

A non-stick pan is a useful invention which makes our cooking lives much easier, however it is important to be aware that the non-stick coating on a pan contains PFCs. This chemical is released from non-stick pans if they are heated at too high a temperature (especially if dry) or if they are scratched. Animal studies have shown exposure to PFCs to cause toxic effects including negative reproductive and developmental effects. You can limit your exposure to this chemical by using alternative types of pans or by ensuring you take care not to scratch your pan and to replace it when it does become scratched.

Smoking

Of course, we all know that smoking is bad for us, whether or not we choose to smoke. Tobacco smoke contains around 7,000 chemicals. Many of these chemicals are poisonous and over 60 are carcinogenic (they are known to cause cancer). Chemicals in tobacco smoke include nicotine, tar, carbon monoxide, arsenic (found in rat poison), ammonia (commonly found in cleaning products), acetone (a solvent found in nail polish remover) and methanol (aviation fuel). Aside from cancer, chronic bronchitis and the multitude of other health issues we know stem from smoking cigarettes, the physical effects of addiction and withdrawal to nicotine can also be incredibly stressful on the body and mind.

Cleaning products and Glycol ethers

If you read the back of your kitchen and bathroom cleaning products you will likely be looking at a very long list. Unless you are one of the chemists amongst us, many of the chemicals will be unfamiliar to you. These products can also often be labelled as harmful, toxic or sometimes fatal when ingested or touched. That pungent smell from your oven cleaner occurs because some very strong chemicals are at play.

Glycol ethers are a chemical commonly found in cleaning products, liquid soaps and cosmetics. Acute exposure can result in, amongst other things, kidney and liver damage and pulmonary oedema, while long-term exposure to these chemicals can cause conditions such as fatigue, nausea and tremors to name a few.

Consider avoiding using products that list Glycol ethers in the ingredients list and please be aware that Glycol ethers can be listed under many name variants on products labels.

Often, we do not need harmful chemicals to clean effectively; vinegar, lemon, baking soda and good old soap and water can often do the trick.

BPA

You have probably heard of BPA or seen the term 'BPA Free' on labels for plastic bottles. BPA (Bisphenol A) is found in plastic and the lining of food tins and is even sometimes found in the till receipt you take from the shop.

BPA can affect behaviour as well as your brain and the National Institutes of Environmental Health Sciences (NIEHS) notes animal studies have shown negative effects in newborns and foetuses after exposure to BPA.

BPA can leach into food when plastic containers are heated up or into food when it is stored in aluminium tins. It is advised to heat and store food in alternative containers such as glass or stainless steel and to look for a 'BPA free' label when buying plastic bottles and containers.

Mercury

Fish is an incredibly healthy source of Omega-3 fatty acids and can certainly be enjoyed as a healthy part of an omnivorous diet. However, it is important to be aware that some varieties of fish can contain high levels of mercury. Species of fish such as shark, swordfish, king mackerel and other fish higher up the food chain contain higher amounts. These species tend to eat the smaller fish and these smaller fish contain low levels of mercury, which in turn causes the larger fish to have increased levels of mercury.

The risk from mercury can be especially high for young children, pregnant women and the developing foetus. It is recommended that you limit your intake of these top-of-the-food-chain fish and instead enjoy varieties of fish lower in mercury, such as salmon, cod and BPA free tinned light tuna.

This is just a small snapshot of the chemicals we encounter in our day-to-day lives. Chemicals are so much part of our everyday life it is impossible to completely avoid them. However, I want you to feel informed and empowered. I want you to be more aware of the products you use and the effects that these can have on your body and well-being. I want you to be armed with information so you can make the healthiest choices available for yourself and the people you care about.

Please have a look in your home and your cupboards. What products do you use? Is there something less harmful that would do the job just as well? What small changes could you make to improve your health?

Nutritional Stress

Ann Wigmore, holistic health practitioner and raw food advocate originally expressed the idea that "the food you eat can be either the safest and most powerful form of medicine or the slowest form of poison." You will hear me come back to this phrase a few times throughout this book because I believe it so strongly. What we choose to feed ourselves can build us up or it can break us down.

Every day we make choices about food. What to eat for breakfast? Do I have time to eat this morning? Sandwich or leftovers for lunch? What do I want more, an apple or a chocolate bar? I'm thirsty, what shall I drink? Shall I try that new recipe I saw on the T.V. last night? Shall I order a takeaway, or shall I have a salad?

Food is almost constantly on our minds and our food choices make a huge difference to the level of stress we place on our body. This is because some food that we eat can energise and invigorate us and some food can be pro-inflammatory or have little or no nutritional value. Food can in fact be detrimental to our health.

I have interviewed a number of nutritionists and there appears to be a common theme. When they have a client with an autoimmune condition or a chronic inflammatory condition, they will often recommend that the client removes gluten, dairy, wheat and soy from their diet.

Let's look at gluten. Gluten is a binding agent which does not have any nutritional value of its own. Some people suffer from Coeliac Disease, an allergy to gluten which causes an autoimmune response from the body, leading to pain and long-term damage to the gut lining. Other people may have gluten intolerance, where they cannot digest gluten properly and this leads to discomfort and inflammation of the gut lining.

However, and this is the most important point, NO PERSON is designed to digest gluten. Take this example to illustrate this. Some plants require animals to ingest their seeds so they can be taken to a different location to be germinated. Gluten is the casing around a seed and when that seed is eaten by an animal, it is the gluten that stops that seed from being digested. This is so the animal can excrete that seed and it can be fertilized as the plant intended.

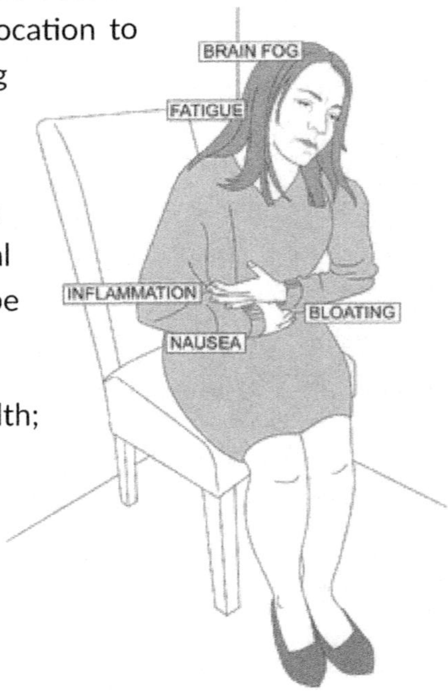

Gluten has an impact on our health; short-term it can cause bloating and discomfort and long term it can negatively impact the absorption of some nutrients. This can cause symptoms such as nausea, fatigue, brain fog and inflammation.

Similarly, dairy products have an adverse effect on a huge number of people. Approximately 65 percent of the human population has a reduced ability to digest lactose after infancy. Lactose intolerance in adulthood is most prevalent in people of East Asian descent, affecting more than 90 percent of adults in some of these communities. The prevalence of lactose intolerance is lowest in populations with a long history of dependence on unfermented milk products as an important food source. For example, only about 5 percent of people of Northern European descent are lactose intolerant.[2]

Therefore, the majority of us may well have an adverse reaction to dairy products which puts stress on our body, but many of us may not be aware that the way we feel is not 'normal'.

As previously mentioned, nutritionists will often ask clients suffering from inflammatory or autoimmune conditions to remove gluten, wheat, dairy and soy from their diet and then when symptoms have improved, to add them slowly back one by one. This allows the client and nutritionist to note which food brings about a return of their symptoms and an inflammatory response from the body. It can take time for symptoms to improve as it can take a number of weeks for the body to heal itself after inflammation.

We will look at nutrition in much more detail in Part 4 – Performance and Fuel to THRIVE®, however, we will briefly look at some nutritional stresses that our body can suffer dependent on the food choices we make.

In our modern diet, we have a habit of overcooking food and when foods containing fats and oils are cooked at high temperatures, they can become oxidized. This creates free radicals. To explain, when

---

2 Genetics Home Reference, *Lactose Intolerance*, 2010 <https://ghr.nlm.nih.gov/condition/lactose-intolerance#statistics>

oxygen splits into single atoms with unpaired electrons (electrons like to be in pairs) these atoms, which we call free radicals, seek out other electrons in the body that they can pair with. This action causes damage to cells, proteins and DNA. This damage from free radicals has been associated with a number of diseases including cancer and Alzheimer's Disease.

Vitamins and minerals are designed to mop up free radicals but often we have a depleted level of vitamins and minerals in our body due either to choosing less nutritionally rich food or because of the depleted level of vitamins and minerals in what we eat. This can be due to the quality of modern farming soil (we will discuss this in more detail in Part 4).

We also consume far too much processed sugar which puts stress on our bodies. When we eat sugar there is a surge of dopamine (the feel-good chemical) in our brain, this leads to stressful sugar cravings and our desire to eat more and MORE. Also, when we eat sugar, sugar-loving bacteria thrive in our bodies and they release neuropeptides, which are chemical messengers that demand more sugar from your brain and so the cycle continues and the bad bacteria can thrive.

Consumption of sugar can cause stress on the pancreas. If we eat excessive levels of sugar, our body develops an insulin resistance and the pancreas needs to work overtime to make more and more insulin. Eventually your pancreas can no longer keep up and begins to break down leading to the symptoms of Type 2 diabetes.

Low-grade chronic inflammation in the body can be caused by a combination of nutritional stress, as described above, physical stress caused by over-exercising or repetitive strain injury or emotional stress and the continued effects of the release of stress hormones. If you have a combination of different factors in your life creating inflammation, then this can lead your body to not function at its best and cause pain or health problems.

The food we choose to put into our bodies is one of the most powerful decisions we make every day. When we deprive our body of the right food, symptoms of nutritional stress can include weight gain, fatigue, depression, palpitations, dry mouth and digestive issues. It can also lead to diseases such as diabetes, heart disease or cancer. When your body is not assimilating and absorbing the correct nutrients or it is having to work harder to do so, this places your body under stress.

I encourage you to choose your food and eat it in a mindful way, to be aware of the food choices you are making and how they make your body feel.

Understanding the body's nutritional and dietary needs is a big part of my work with my patients. When a patient tells me they have a 'healthy diet' it is important for me to understand what healthy means to them. A healthy diet is complex and when we look at their diet in more detail together there are often areas that they can improve. We will look at this more closely in Part 4.

Environmental Stress

Just as with Chemical Stress, we encounter Environmental Stress as a part of our day-to-day lives. The air we breathe, the light and sounds around us and the technology we use can all affect our environment. When the environment we are living in is less than ideal it can have short and long-term effects on our health and well-being. Here are just a few common stresses created by our environment.

Lighting

The light quality you live and work in can have an effect on physical and mental health. Poor lighting, whether that be lights that are too bright or too dim or a poor and flickering quality of light such as fluorescent tubes, can cause stress on our bodies. It can have adverse effects on our health including eye strain and fatigue. For people with light sensitivity, flickering or poor-quality lighting can cause headaches and migraine. Poor light quality can also have an effect on our emotions making us feel anxious or giving us a general feeling of 'stress', which can affect our productivity.

Using phones, tablets and other screens prior to going to bed has been shown to affect sleep. Blue light emitted by screens reduces the level of melatonin produced by your body. Melatonin is the hormone that controls your sleep and wake rhythms and by reducing it, your brain is more alert and this makes it harder to fall asleep and stay asleep.

Try to make your bedroom a peaceful, technology-free zone, a place where you can relax and unwind. If this isn't possible, then make sure you have at least thirty-minutes 'screen-free' before you go to sleep.

Noise

We are constantly surrounded by noise. Silence outside of the vacuum of space is impossible. Whether it is the sound of traffic, a noisy neighbour or even the hum of your boiler in the background, unsettling sounds in our environment can have damaging effects to our health, potentially leading to sleep disturbance and insomnia, memory problems and fatigue. Noise pollution can also lead to mental health problems such as depression, especially if it continues over an extended period.

Acute exposure to noise pollution such as through use of heavy machinery at work or at a deafening concert can also cause serious damage to your eardrums.

Sun

The sun has dangers and also benefits. Natural light has been shown to improve our mood. Over the winter months when the sun is limited in the UK, many people suffer from Seasonal Affective Disorder (SAD), symptoms of which include low mood and depression. The sun also helps our body produce Vitamin D, so it is important to get moderate sun exposure on as much bare skin as possible each day; around twenty minutes of sun exposure on bare skin before applying sunscreen is recommended dependent on your skin tone.

Around 70% of the UK population are deficient in Vitamin D and we will speak about the potential benefits of supplementation in Part 4. Vitamin D plays a huge role in immune function, hormone regulation, bone health and tissue and muscle function.

However, the sun also poses environmental dangers including sunburn and skin cancer. As we know, it is important to cover up, use sunscreen and stay out of the sun during the hottest part of the day and for extended periods to help protect our bodies.

Too much ultraviolet (UV) radiation from the sun can damage DNA in your skin cells and cause skin cancer. In the UK, almost 9 in 10 cases of melanoma, the most serious type of skin cancer, could be prevented through enjoying the sun safely and avoiding the use of sunbeds. Getting sunburnt just once every 2 years can triple your risk of melanoma skin cancer.[3]

---

3 Cancer Research UK, *How does the sun and UV cause cancer?*, 2019 <https://www.cancerresearchuk.org/about-cancer/causes-of-cancer/sun-uv-and-cancer/how-does-the-sun-and-uv-cause-cancer>

Pollution

Pollution encompasses a large number of things including, water, air, soil, thermal, radioactive, noise and light pollution. All of these things have an effect on your environment. So, let us consider air pollution. This can be caused by emissions and the use of fossil fuels. The quality of air in large cities in measurably poorer than that in more rural areas. There is also a seasonal effect on air quality, with pollen causing misery during the summer months for many hay fever sufferers.

Air pollution can increase the risk of a heart attack, breathing problems, coughing, wheezing and asthma. It can also lead to irritation and cause inflammation. An article in The Lancet has highlighted a link between air pollution and neurological disorders, with possible links to diseases of the nervous system as an emerging concern requiring further research.[4]

Wi-Fi, 5G and Electromagnetic fields

Wi-Fi and mobile phones, including 5G technology, create electromagnetic fields (EMFs). We are surrounded by these EMFs both inside and outside our homes. 5G technology uses higher frequency waves than earlier mobile networks, this allows faster speeds and access for more devices. These waves travel a shorter distance than previous mobile technology and therefore require more masts closer to the ground in order to operate.

Professor Denis Henshaw from the University of Bristol and Dr Roger Coghill recently highlighted research suggesting that our brain cannot tell the difference between electromagnetic fields and light waves.

4 The Lancet Neurology, 'Air pollution and brain health: an emerging issue', *The Lancet*, 17, no.2 (2018), p.103

Therefore, when we are constantly surrounded by Wi-Fi, mobile networks and other EMFs our brain believes it is in a constant state of daytime. This seriously affects our body's ability to create melatonin and our body's ability to heal and repair is reduced.

I mentioned melatonin when discussing reducing our screen time, as decreased levels of this hormone can affect our sleep. The pineal gland in our brain is responsible for its production and in order to do this it senses when there is no light. Melatonin is only produced by our body at night, which is the time our body heals and repairs itself and the brain cannot create this hormone when it senses light. Melatonin is also a powerful antioxidant in our body which 'mops up' free radicals which are widely known to be a key player in the creation of cancer cells. As well as affecting our sleep/wake cycle, reduced melatonin can also affect the strength of our immune system and our heart health.

We cannot control how governments will use and implement 5G and other EMF creating technology. There is varied and controversial debate on this topic and perhaps more research needs to be done in this area. In the same way that it is important to limit your screen time before bed, due to the effect of light on your health, it is also important to turn off Wi-Fi and remove mobile phones from the bedroom. How many of us sleep with our phone under our pillow or beside the bed? Make your bedroom a sanctuary, where your brain and body can rest, digest and heal in darkness.

Environmental Stress, like many of the 5 Dimensions of Stress is built into modern day living. It is important to take a look at your home environment and your work environment and take stock of what you can do to reduce any environmental stresses around you that cause you physical or mental stress.

SUMMARY

Now we have looked at the 5 Dimensions of Stress you can see there are a number of ways Physical, Emotional, Chemical, Nutritional and Environmental Stresses can affect us on a day-to-day basis. Prevention is better than cure, so rather than waiting until you have a health condition that has been caused by the long-term effects of stress, which in some cases can be irreversible damage, think about what you can do to reduce these stresses and take action. In this day and age, although you are subject to exposure to some of these stresses on a daily basis, the best balance is achieved by being aware of this and taking steps and measures to reduce the effects of this stress as much as you can.

Please visit my resources section at www.5tothrive.co.uk to download the full '5 Dimensions of Stress workbook'

SCAN ME

So now you have a deeper understanding of how the 5 Dimensions of Stress has an effect you, let's now look deeper at the 5 key areas to focus on to really improve the quality of your health and enable you to THRIVE!

PART 1:
POWER UP

Get in S.Y.N.C.™

Power is the first step to thriving. There are various definitions of power, such as 'knowledge is power'. For your health, your power is your Central Nervous System because it controls everything. Your Central Nervous System controls every cell, every tissue and every organ in your body. Having the energy and ability to reach your goals derives from this system. It's basically the electricity that runs our body, a vast central communication network that carries messages between the brain and body.

This powerful network can be interrupted and put under pressure by The 5 Dimensions of Stress. Dr John Demartini said that "stress is the inability to adapt to a changing environment." Our bodies have not necessarily had the time to evolve to cope well with the environment that we live in today. Society evolves at a faster rate than our genes have time to adapt. Therefore, our hunter-gatherer genetics struggle to cope with the stresses of this modern society. Every day, we might sleep in a bed that's too soft, spend hours at a desk for example, or lift something up that's too heavy and cause back injuries, or we can have a car accident or a slip or fall, putting our body under a great deal of stress. We're living in a 'nano-second culture' that bombards us with information that our brain has to work hard to filter out. All of this extra work for the body and brain causes us stress, putting strain on both our immune system and our health.

Connection - The nervous system is like your phones network

Take your mobile phone, for example. You would do anything you could to get a signal to send and receive messages. You might even lean out of a window or stand on a chair trying to get the best conditions for a clear signal. Well, why don't we make the same effort for the messages in our body? Why do we pop pills or take painkillers, rather than striving to receive and translate the messages our body is struggling to send? Symptoms are the way our body signals to us that something isn't right. It's easy to become disconnected from our body's communication network, our Central Nervous System. Power is about restoring that connection. In the words of B.J. Palmer, the 'Developer of Chiropractic', "the power that makes the body, heals the body."

The body has an innate intelligence and is designed to heal and repair itself. Under the right conditions, the body can heal itself and this is what chiropractors aim to nurture. It's not the plaster cast that heals a fracture, it's the bone cells that move in, clear the debris and fuse the fracture site. They are designed to do that. How does the body know how to do this? It comes from the body's inborn wisdom called 'innate intelligence'. The body has an inner know-how, an inbuilt organisation and it knows exactly how to perform at its best.

Sometimes we can get a chronic injury or illness which the body doesn't heal and we then need to look at why it's not healing. Sometimes it's because the stress that caused the problem is still there. The root of the problem hasn't been solved. If you had a scab and kept knocking it off, it's not going to heal properly, or it will take much longer than it should. It's the same if you're doing something that repetitively strains your body. If you have postural problems, this is not good for your body and it is going to affect how well it works. If your nerves are irritated, inflamed or under pressure they also won't work as well. In turn, this affects your nervous system and the innate intelligence of your body. In the excellent book 'The Power of Self-Healing' by Dr Fabrizio Mancini he explores further how the body has the incredible capacity to heal and repair itself.

Power is about tapping into your body's innate intelligence. It's about understanding the centrality of your Central Nervous System in controlling every cell, tissue and organ in your body and harnessing your body's capacity to heal itself and maintain optimal health.

Your Central Nervous System connects your brain and body and is a little bit like the electrical wiring in a house. An electrician wires up a house, with cables running into the plug sockets and lighting points in all of your rooms. The wires that service your plug or switch are like the spinal nerves in your body. You can connect an extension cable to your plug socket and run other appliances off it. This works in a similar way to nerve roots, which branch off from the spinal cord (a critical part of the Central Nervous System) and run throughout your body, providing a path for messages from the brain to travel to peripheral regions of the body, such as the arms and legs.

This enables us to walk, run and perform other everyday activities. Therefore, if you have a problem with the spine, the messages between your brain and body can get interfered with, causing pain, numbness or tingling in other areas of your body, such as your arms or legs. This is a bit like when there's a fault with the electrical wiring in your house and the light-bulb flickers or an appliance stops working. You could have, for example, a disc injury or a bone spur that's irritating, inflaming, or even compressing the nerve. If the nerve is badly compressed it may result in needing surgery to take pressure off. However, chiropractors are often able to treat and manage these cases extremely well by actually working with the spine and influencing the nervous system, helping to restore those messages.

> "90% of the stimulation and nutrition to the brain is generated by the movement of the spine.
>
> \- Dr Roger Sperry
>
> *Nobel Prize Laureate 1981 for Split Brain research.*

In order to Power Up and enable your body to heal and repair itself to the best of its ability, you need to get in S. Y. N. C.

S – Symptoms

Y – You

N – Neurology

C – Chiropractic

This is a formula I follow with my patients. The first step is really key because it allows us both to understand and translate the messages that your nervous system is giving you. This is the foundational step in getting to THRIVE. The **'S'** I am describing is your **S**ymptoms.

Symptoms

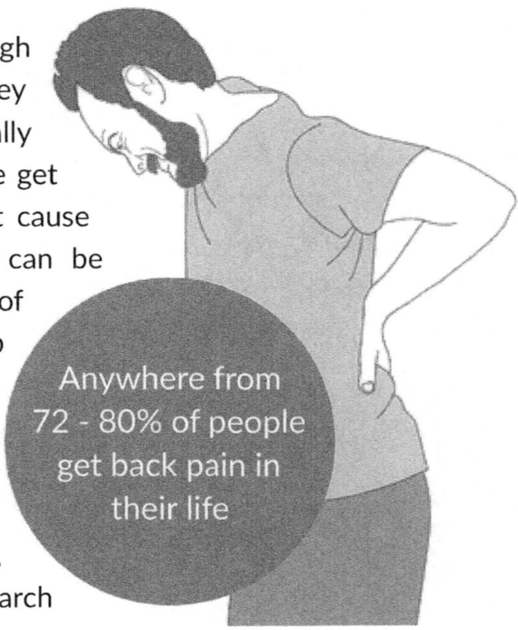

Why is it that even though people want to THRIVE, they fall into patterns that actually don't lead to it? Well, people get into certain habits. The root cause of many health challenges can be found in The 5 Dimensions of Stress. So, people develop habits relating to these five key stresses that affect their body on a day-to-day basis and can result in pain and/or injury. Take back pain, for example. Current research compiled by my colleague Dr Niels Peter Carstens demonstrates that approximately 80% of people get back pain in their life, which is huge. 60% of these people get a recurrence of an injury, around 40% of those people get multiple re-injuries and out of that, 20% end up in chronic pain, so they're getting gradually worse over time. [5]

Like a detective working through clues, your symptoms will help us understand and diagnose the cause of the problem.

Pain – symptom or cause?

Pain is a message from your nervous system that gets detected in the brain. It's part of your warning system that tells you that there is a problem. There are different types and ways of describing pain: dull, achy, sharp, shooting, stabbing, pinching, catching, burning, tooth-achy, referred, acute or chronic.

For example, a common, mild version could be a twinge in your lower back as you transition from sitting to standing or turning over in bed. If this area becomes progressively worse, a twinge turns into a catch or pinch and worse still is a stabbing or knife-like pain.

Taking painkillers can mask the pain and help to get someone mobile again in the short-term but it doesn't address the problem, leaving people in danger of having a relapse. If you're ignoring the messages and doing things your body is telling you not to do, it could even get worse. Take back pain as an example. In an article published in the medical journal the Lancet, it states that there is an inappropriately high amount of medications, injections and surgery used in the treatment of back pain.

---

5 Devon I. Rubin, 'Epidemiology and Risk Factors for Spine Pain', *Neurologic Clinics*, 25, no.2 (2007), pp.353-371
J.K. Freburger et al., 'The Rising Prevalence of Chronic Low Back Pain', *Archives of Internal Medicine*, 169, no.3 (2009), pp.251–258
Nadine E. Foster et al., 'Prevention and Treatment of low back pain: evidence, challenges and promising directions', The Lancet, 391, no.10137 (2018) pp.2368-2383

It's important to identify what the pain means by listening to your body. Is it a problem when you're sitting? Is it when you're bending? As chiropractors, one of the things we do is really understand and interpret the language of pain, which in turn can help us locate the cause of the problem. Someone might say, 'I have a burning pain', 'I have numbness', 'I can feel a dull tooth-achy pain', or 'I have a sharp stabbing pain'. All of those mean different things. In the previous example, if you have sharp stabbing lower back pain when you go from sitting to standing and turning in bed, the odds are that you might have a facet or sacroiliac sprain/strain injury. Whereas if you have a horrible, burning, tooth-achy pain that's going down the side of the leg or down through the buttock into the lower thigh, it could be a sign that the sciatic nerve is irritated and that can sometimes be from a disc problem or from an arthritic change. Obviously, I would never offer a diagnosis conclusively until I'd assessed somebody thoroughly and talked to them about their experience, however the point is that we can tell a great deal by listening to your body and interpreting and translating the language of pain. The messages that the body is giving enables us to understand and help diagnose what's going on.

Chiropractic adjustments reboot and reset the nervous system and in turn, this recalibrates muscle balance, which will strengthen the weak muscle and soften the tight muscle and, in most cases, allow an area to heal. One of my patients, for example, had a martial arts injury where, when kicking, they slipped and fell onto their backside. After the accident, other than having back pain, they noticed that their legs felt heavy (this is due to a partial loss of power and strength in the leg muscles). They went to their doctor and had an MRI. The MRI came back with a normal result, yet they still had this heavy feeling in their legs.

When he came to be checked at our chiropractic wellness centre, I performed some assessments and tests and found that when gentle pressure was placed on the spine in a specific direction it restored the feeling of power into his legs. Over time and with a course of gentle, specific adjustments, this improvement continued. I had another patient, Richard, with a similar issue. He had seen eight other professionals and said he felt a weakness in his muscles every time he bent forward and his back 'went out'. It was affecting his ability to do his work, play basketball and even worse, play with his children. Again, after a series of adjustments he felt the power switching back on in his muscles and was able to stabilise his back and get back to all the activities that he was missing out on.

Symptoms can be complicated and difficult to interpret. They don't always directly relate to health problems in a straightforward way - they can have knock on effects. For example, physical stress can also affect your nervous system and can slow your cognitive process, cause tiredness, weaken your immune system and make you more likely to experience a fall or injury. 21st century stress can cause physical effects on the body that you may not be able to see. When you have either chronic pain or emotional stress, the body's immune system functions can become suppressed. Stress hormones impair nerve function, which can cause excess glucose in the brain and even shrink the hippocampus (which is responsible for learning and memory). Cortisol (a stress hormone) also slows the metabolism and triggers fat storage. In other words, the stress response can actually affect your memory and increase your fat storage and therefore affect your ability to achieve a healthy weight. Chronic stress can also lead to high blood pressure, erratic blood sugar and high cholesterol.

To avoid chronic stress, it is really important that you understand where your symptoms relating to the 5 Dimensions of Stress might be coming from.

To recap:

Physical Stress, as described earlier, could be coming from posture, repetitive strain, trauma, twisting, injuries, to name a few. Symptoms could also include low energy, nausea, pain, weakness, numbness, tingling, pins and needles, headaches and tense muscles.

Emotional Stress from our environment, relationships, finances, health or even the thoughts we have causes us to fire off the stress response or use unhealthy coping habits or behaviours to bring about a change in state such as smoking, drinking, comfort eating or anger.

Depending on the level of severity and duration of the stress, this will lead to changes in our thoughts, patterns and behaviours both in the short and long term. Identifying your symptoms, behaviours and habits is the first step to create change.

I am sure you would agree if you can take a dis-empowering stress pattern of behaviour and replace it with a healthy one, this small shift can have significant positive outcomes for your health.

Emotional stress often causes headaches and fatigue, which can be mistaken for physical stress. Fear, anxiety, anger and frustrations are just some of the emotions that can lead to a release of neurochemicals and stress hormones in the fight-or-flight response. Often, people seek medication as a method of relief; however, relief is usually only temporary and does not remove the underlying cause of the problem. When we get to the Mind Mastery Matrix® section, I will go through empowering and healthy ways to reduce the effects of the stress response.

Chemical Stress could come from a number of areas such as smoking, pollution, household products, deodorants or prescription medications. The effects of these chemicals getting into your body can become stored in your fat cells or circulate in your blood stream which eventually leads to long-term health problems.

Nutritional Stress can be caused by the food you eat. Meals with little or no nutritional value can result in internal stress on our organs. Food can be the best form of medicine for your body or the worst form of poison. Symptoms of nutritional stress could be weight gain, fatigue, depression, palpitations, bloating, dry mouth, constipation, diarrhoea, or diseases such as diabetes, heart disease or cancer.

Environmental Stress could be a result of Wi-Fi, noise, light levels or radiation as it surrounds us during daily life. The impact of environmental stress in the long-term can lead to insomnia, headaches, the stress response and other health challenges.

It can be overwhelming to try to remove all aspects of stress at the same time. My advice would be to choose 1-3 areas to focus on and take daily and consistent action steps to improve your situation. Once this has been successful, you can move on to work on other areas of stress. Having your health and mind in better balance will give you resilience and some of the other stressors that you haven't worked on yet might not affect you in the same way as before.

As mentioned earlier, to reduce stress in your day-to-day life you really need to identify the aggravating factors, then decide which relieving factors you can apply to lessen the impact.

As chiropractors, we find that identifying and understanding symptoms in terms of the 5 Dimensions of Stress is incredibly powerful. It enables us to help each patient as an individual when performing examinations and making our recommendations and diagnosis. This helps to clarify possible underlying causes and we can then give specific lifestyle advice. We can also identify ways to avoid recreating or even continuing with the stresses that contributed to the problem in the first place.

This brings us onto the next key step in getting your system in S.Y.N.C.™ and that is YOU.

YOU

You have so much control over your health, probably even more than you realise. People can get so used to feeling tired and having aches and pains that it becomes their 'norm'. Once you understand how your body works, you can really start to THRIVE. It's about taking charge of your health. If you feel okay, but you regularly smoke and drink, or you know that you're eating bad food, please don't tell yourself that you're healthy, because you know that really, deep down you're not. It's about being honest with yourself and taking your health seriously. The worst case is that too many people often leave changing unhealthy habits until it's too late. I like to remind myself of this by asking the question, 'what are you pretending not to know?'

Recently, I was talking to my friend, Neil Martin, the 'Natural Juice Junkie', about the current crisis that seems to be prevalent, which we named 'the ostrich epidemic'. There's a growing number of people throughout the world who choose to bury their heads in the sand rather than deal with reality. Their problems won't go away just because they ignore them.

When it comes to health, most people have some level of understanding of foods, behaviours and decisions that will promote health and those that will reduce health. Just understanding this is not enough - you need to take action. Most people find it difficult to change the habits of a lifetime. When it comes to YOU, your beliefs, ideas, thoughts and behaviours come from either your parents, your education, your culture or the environment that has shaped you. This blueprint of the world gives us both our successes and failures in life. However, it is not impossible to improve your situation if you have the right help and strategies in your tool kit. Often with the right help you could also improve things much more quickly than you perhaps realise.

If where you are right now in your health is challenged, stressed and overwhelmed, the good news is making small progressive steps towards health can make a huge difference. On the other hand, if you would consider yourself healthy, then you can use this book as a guide to fine-tune your wellness.

Before you began to read this book, when was the last time you actually paused to reflect deeply about your health choices? The greatest gift that you have is the ability and power to make changes, even if they start off as small steps.

The key thing, as you'll learn throughout this book, is committing to your health, because when you're committed enough to something, you find a way to do it. Even if it's not the perfect way, even if it's not the way that's going to get you to your destination in the quickest possible time, that doesn't matter because doing something is better than doing nothing.

There's much more to your health than you might initially think. Your health and decisions that you make about it are unique to you. All changes that you want to make start from within. Just take a minute now to imagine a healthy person. What comes to mind? A physically fit body maybe, or a bowl of salad and a kale smoothie? The fuel you put into your body is obviously very important to your health, however the thoughts and beliefs in your mind are equally important.

Think back to a time when you were experiencing stress and it had a physical and mental effect on you and the people around you. How did it make you feel? How did it impact the people around you? Now, ask yourself this; what can you do to protect yourself from stress? That's an important question, which we'll return to at the end of the book, by which time, you should be able to list several actions you can take.

Exercise

I recommend you find a quiet place to complete this exercise. Pull out your health journal and answer the following questions.

- Is health important to me?
- Why is health important?
- What do I need to change to move towards health?
- What are my health goals for the next...
- One year?
- One quarter?
- One month?
- One week?
- And what one thing can I do specifically **TODAY** to move towards these goals?
- What do I need to do more of, less of, change or stop to achieve a better quality of life?

I always say:

You do not need to be healthy to begin; you need to begin to be healthy.

How much action you take always comes down to the decisions you make and the level of importance you place on your health. Changing your mindset towards living a healthier life can drastically improve your chances of reaching your health goals.

Here's the thing; your health affects everything you do and everyone you know and YOU are too important not to take action to move towards a healthier future. Becoming inspired about your health and your future health is the spark to drive change.

Neurology

The nervous system is the master controlling system.

We discussed earlier that the brain and nervous system control every cell, tissue and organ in our body. So, let's now dive deeper.

Dr Heidi Haavik, leading researcher in neuroscience and chiropractic, has conducted in depth research in this area and I would like to highlight some of her work here.[6]

The body functions by continually sending information to the brain and back again, this communicates information to the brain about your body and the environment you are in. Our body utilises sensory organs to send these messages via our nerves. If we take the ear, for example, when sound waves enter the ear, the eardrum vibrates and this is then sent as a message to the brain, which is decoded and

6 *Your Brain, Body and Spine* [animation video], created by Dr Heidi Haavik (Haavik Research Limited, n.d.)

translated into what you hear. Another sensory organ, the eye, detects light at the back of the retina, a message is sent via the optic nerve to the brain where the information is then interpreted as what we can see. We are all familiar with the five senses, sight, hearing, smell, taste and touch, but did you know that muscles are also sensory organs?

Our muscles send messages to the brain regarding spatial awareness of where our limbs are in time and space, this is known as proprioception (the body's balancing and positioning sense). Surrounding the spine, there are muscles called paraspinal muscles, which are incredibly important, they tell the brain what your spine is doing and where your head, neck and body are through the sense proprioception.

When you have an injury or if the spinal segments aren't moving in a functional way, perhaps due to poor posture, the communication between your paraspinal muscles and your brain gets distorted and as a result muscle tension, muscle spasm and weakness can exist. This creates imbalance within the joints and a strain can start to affect ligaments. If your spinal segments aren't moving properly, your brain may not get the information it needs about what is happening in your body and will therefore have to fill in the blanks. If your brain is not fully aware of what is going on in your body you will also be more susceptible to injury.

Dr Heidi Haavik uses the following analogy:

"Imagine for a moment that you've lived in a house all your life and that in this house there is a long corridor with no windows. At the end of the corridor is an electrical fuse box. Now imagine that the circuit breaker to the lights has blown and you are pitched into complete darkness. Would you be completely helpless, or could you walk down that corridor and turn the circuit breaker back on? Of course, you could. You've lived there all your life. You would know roughly how long the corridor was and how wide it was. You would be able to get down there and turn the lights back on. Your brain is just as smart as that. It can function even if there's parts of the body that it cannot see. It will be able to function and control those parts of your body because of its past experience, but now imagine that before those lights went out your kids had left a bicycle in that long corridor that you had not seen. What would happen in that scenario? You would likely fall and hurt yourself and this is what happens when the brain is not fully aware of what is going on somewhere in your body or in your environment. You could end up having an accident or hurt yourself."[7]

This fantastic analogy helps us to understand that your brain sees every part of your body and if messages become distorted due to dysfunction within the spinal segments, the brain is unable to see clearly. An interesting example shows how movements are so intrinsically coordinated with our brain. If you hear a loud sound, a reflex occurs from your ear to your accessory muscles and you will turn your head and eyes, sometimes before you are even aware that you have heard something. This reflex shows the coordination between hearing and neck movements. If you have had a neck or whiplash injury, you can get a mismatch of firing which can create muscle spasm and tension, which can in turn affect hearing, balance and proprioception, sometimes leading to light headedness and headaches.

---

7 *Your Brain, Body and Spine* [animation video], created by Dr Heidi Haavik (Haavik Research Limited, n.d.)

When chiropractors assess the spine, they are looking for these dysfunctional segments that may be affecting the signal between your body and brain. Chiropractors use the term 'vertebral subluxation' to describe the area that is dysfunctional. When a chiropractor performs a chiropractic adjustment, which is a gentle force to the area, it effectively acts as a reboot to the signal and the connection between body and brain. If spinal segments have been dysfunctional for an extended period it can sometimes take a number of sessions to reboot and retrain, in the same way as going to the gym, it takes time to build up strength by repetition, you need to retrain your muscles and connections. When chiropractors adjust the spine, as well as freeing up movements and getting the body to move and function better, adjustments also restore normal movement, allowing the body to heal and repair itself. The aim is to get the nervous system coordinating, functioning and firing on a much better level.

When your brain can accurately perceive what is going on inside and out it can better control your body for the situation at hand and move muscles in the right order. This means your body moves accurately, you have fewer accidents and you can function and perform at your best.

THREE PARTS OF THE CENTRAL NERVOUS SYSTEM

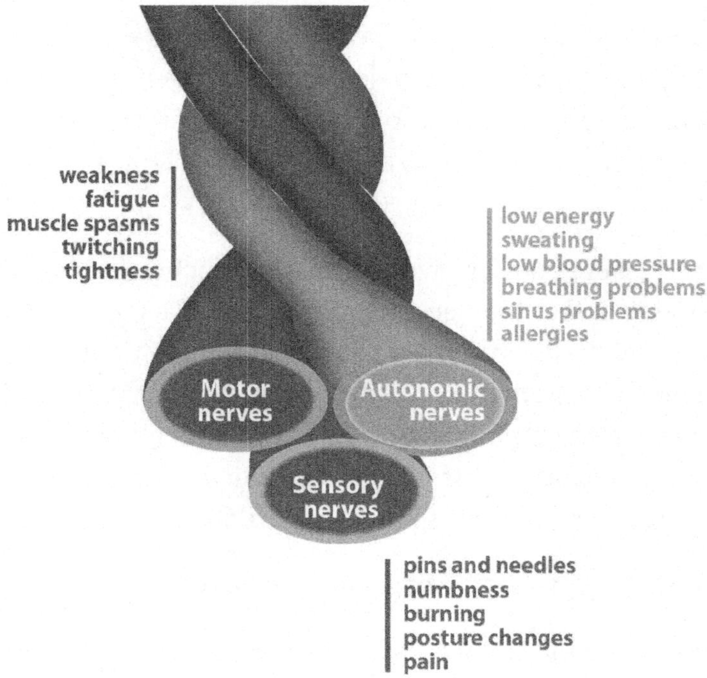

	Function	Symptoms from nerve interference
Motor Nerves	Control muscles	Weakness, fatigue, muscle spasms, twitching and tightness
Autonomic Nerves	Control organs, glands and blood vessels	Low energy, sweating, low blood pressure, breathing problems, sinus problems and allergies
- Sympathetic	Fight, flight, freeze	
- Parasympathetic	Rest, digest, heal	
Sensory Nerves	Control body and brain communications including pain, temperature and proprioception (joint positioning sense)	Pins and needles, numbness, burning, posture changes and pain

When we look at nerves there are three main components: Sensory, Motor and Autonomic.

Sensory nerve fibres take information to the brain, such as touch, vibration, pain, temperature or joint positioning. If this area becomes affected, we can experience pain, tingling, numbness or clumsiness. Sensory nerve fibres make up only approximately 10% of our nervous system.

The **motor** fibres are involved in muscle function. A muscle cannot do anything unless the nerve signals it to. If this part of the nervous system is affected, we can get a weakness or heaviness, or tightness of muscles. Physiotherapy, pilates, core stability and rehabilitation exercises aim to stretch tight muscles and strengthen weak muscles. One of the unique effects of a chiropractic adjustment is that it will essentially create a reset of the resting balance of the muscle tone.

So how do nerves control resting muscle function?

The resting tension in a muscle is known as tone. If the nerve messages that control a muscle become dysfunctional, the relaxed tension can increase; this is known as hypertonicity and if the relaxed tension decreases, it's known as hypotonicity. In other words, the muscles at rest can become too tight or too weak. If the continuous strain of hypertonic (tight) muscles continues this can lead to inflammation or damage at the tendon insertion point.

Inflammation of tendons is called tendonitis. Examples of this are plantar fasciitis (affecting the sole of the foot), patella femoral pain syndrome (affecting the movement of the kneecap), tennis or golfer's elbow (affecting the tendons in the elbow) or rotator cuff impingement (affecting the shoulder).

When your chiropractor adjusts your spine or joints, one of the effects are that the weak muscles are stimulated and can fire better and the tight muscles soften. This is similar to rebooting a computer. This would allow the muscles to become 'facilitated' thereby improving your success rate with your exercises because you have more effective muscle tone. Also, by softening these hypertonic muscles from an adjustment we often see improvements in tendonitis as the muscle relaxes and reduces the strain allowing the tendon to heal and repair.

The third part of the nervous system is called the 'Autonomic Nervous System'. Think of the **autonomic** nervous system as the **automatic** nervous system.

The autonomic nervous system is one of the most important systems we have in our body as it controls everything else in your body, from organs, to blood vessels, to glands. These nerves are split into two parts. Fight-or-flight is the sympathetic part of the nervous system. Rest, digest and heal is the parasympathetic system.

It is believed that the improvements chiropractors see with some cases of heartburn, headaches, IBS and asthma, to name a few, are due to the improvement in nervous system function in this area.

There is ever increasing research that supports the results chiropractors see in their clinics daily. As chiropractors we do not treat the condition itself (such as headaches), it is through a combination of both adjustments to the spine and lifestyle advice reducing the 5 Dimensions of Stress, that we are able to help our patients with their health goals.

A number of our patients will report better focus, concentration, energy levels and feelings of well-being, as well as reduced pain, better sleep and improved quality of life.

Chiropractic

Chiropractic is an entire health care profession that focuses on the diagnosis, treatment and management of neuromuscular disorders. Through adjusting the spine and other joints chiropractors see the body through the lens of the nervous system.

Chiropractic was founded on the basis that the body is designed to heal and repair itself and the nervous system is the master system that controls everything in our body. Our body has an inborn wisdom called innate intelligence to heal and repair itself. We are affected by the 5 Dimensions of Stress and this causes the spine and joints to become restricted, a little bit like a trip switch on your circuit breaker. This causes what chiropractors often refer to as Vertebral Subluxation, where the misalignment and restriction of the vertebra has an impact on the nerves, either causing local pain around the area or interference with the nerve distorting the messages. The chiropractic adjustment therefore acts like a reboot button so not only does the pain improve but the function of the nervous system is better.

If left uncorrected subluxations and lifestyle stress caused by the 5 Dimensions of Stress, may have a negative effect on your body and your health may degenerate and worsen.

If we correct the subluxations and show you ways to avoid recreating problems in the future you may:

a. Feel better
b. Prevent problems in the future
c. Reverse the effects of the aging process
d. Have a better quality of life

Subluxations are a health problem not a back problem![8]

Chiropractic care draws on the science of neurology to help our patients reduce pain, improve muscle function and live a better quality of life; in other words, THRIVE.

We discussed earlier the different functions of the nervous system. As the nervous system is so complex there are a number of different chiropractic approaches.

Some approaches will be narrow focused for symptomatic relief only. Other approaches look more in depth and once the pain and symptoms have gone or been reduced, there is a focus on optimisation of recovery. This creates stabilisation and improvement in motor function, thus allowing better healing and repair.

Further approaches will take a postural and biomechanical view of coordinating better muscle function in postural muscles and improving biomechanics leading to strengthening and stability for movement,

---

8 Based on the work of Russ Rosen

balance and performance. Another approach observes the effects of the adjustments on the autonomic nervous system and patients have reported reduced stress, improved well-being, better immune system function and reduced symptoms of heartburn, migraines, asthma and improved focus and concentration.

Chiropractors do not have adjustments for specific conditions, rather by checking the function of the spine and adjusting the areas of vertebral subluxations we often see these positive effects from a better functioning nervous system. Your body is designed to heal and repair itself and a healthy nervous system is vital to allow your body to function at optimal levels.

My approach is to meet people where they are at and have a blend of techniques and advice for both short-term and long-term goals. Having worked with patients as young as 4 days old to 99 years young as well as elite athletes and pregnant mums, it is essential to have a varied toolkit to work with each person's individual needs.

If we take the illustration below, known as Panjabi's model for chronic low back pain, we see that trauma or a build-up of microtraumas damage the neural tissues in the body and affect the nervous system's control units. In other words, a combination of damage and/or repetitive injuries affect the nervous system leading to further pain, muscle spasm and inflammation. It is thought that this is how the body responds and the nerve interference caused subsequently leads to chronic pain and joint dysfunction. The research helps us understand the science of how chiropractic adjustments can reset and recalibrate the nerves. However, this is only part of the model as the beneficial effects of chiropractic adjustments are wider than just resetting pain and motor fibres. Correct joint and nerve function is the start of healthy movement and function of the body.

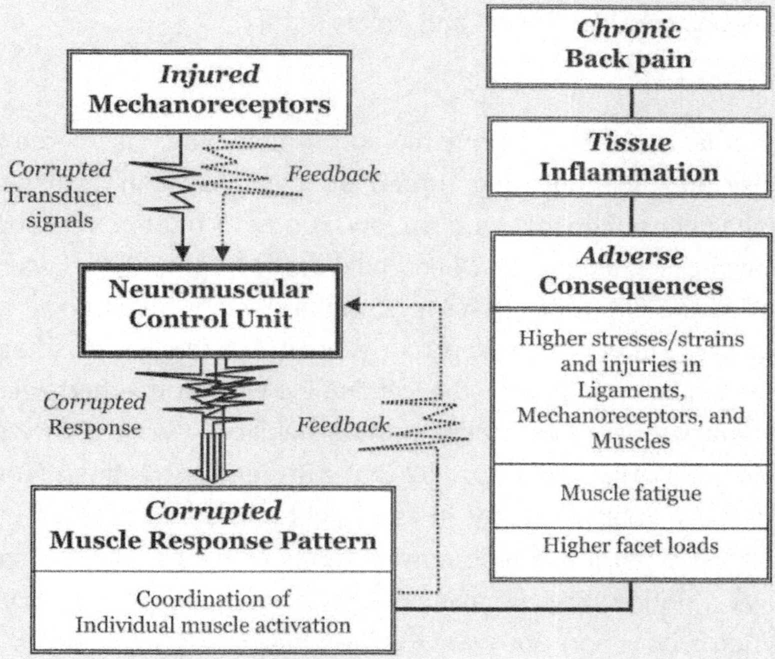

Original source: https://www.ncbi.nlm.nih.gov/pmc/articles/PMC3489327/ FIG 3
Reprinted with thanks from the work by Dr Manohar M. Panjabi
Reference: Manohar M. Panjabi, 'A hypothesis of chronic back pain: ligament subfailure injuries lead to muscle control dysfunction', Eur Spine J, 15, no.5 (2006), pp.668-676

In summary, the mechanoreceptors are pressure sensors in the joint. When the joint dysfunctions this corrupts the signals (messages) from the joints to the positioning sense (proprioception). This leads to abnormal muscle tone around the joints that over time can lead to damage in the area leading to chronic back pain. Another term that you might have heard used to describe this is postural fatigue syndrome.

Now, let us consider Rachel and Archie's story.

"I came to see you about my son, Archie, who has cerebral palsy and had not long turned one. Archie wasn't great at pulling himself up, but within a few months of treatment at your clinic he was able to crawl and hold onto the sofa. There was a noticeable difference in his legs and his weight bearing and he was walking before he was two-years old. He will always have that tendency to lean to the left and we were concerned when he was young about scoliosis and his ability to walk. That was eight years ago now and I feel that with regular treatment, he's grown in a balanced way, in as straight a way as possible. He's quite symmetrical, I feel, now in terms of his gait, he doesn't have a noticeable limp and he's independent in a lot of ways. When he was born, we were told he'd never walk, or would have very serious difficulty walking. But he's going into Year Three now in a mainstream school and he's doing well academically. He's got friends, he takes part in football, taekwondo, swimming and horse riding. He does everything other kids do. I think the chiropractic treatment, along with physiotherapy and speech and language therapy has helped with that. It has given him the confidence to try and I think that's the key."

Some of the exercises that I gave Archie initially were neurological rehabilitation exercises to support the adjustments we were doing. I adjusted his neck and jaw with a gentle percussion instrument to help support the work of his speech therapist and I remember one time he grabbed onto my hair with his hand that we were encouraging him to grab objects with.

Archie's success can partly be explained by neuroplasticity. The brain isn't fixed, you can retrain and rework it. Chiropractic adjustments work to facilitate change alongside physiotherapy and speech and language therapy.

That's what I really love about the principles of chiropractic care - you can keep coming back to them throughout your health. It's about fundamental health - starting with you and your body. It's about being well and tapping into your body's amazing potential to heal itself. Chiropractic care can be used throughout life.

Dr Heidi Haavik has researched in the area of human neurophysiology for the past 15 years. She has used sophisticated brain science techniques to investigate the effects of chiropractic adjustments to vertebral subluxations on various aspects of brain function. I highly recommend her book 'The Reality Check' as an in depth look into the science, research and effects of chiropractic adjustments on improving brain function.

In one specific study[9], Dr Haavik observed how chiropractic adjustments could help people coordinate their body and improve how they perform movements on a daily basis, strengthening the link between their body and brain. The study took a group of twenty-five

---

9 Heidi Haavik and Bernadette Murphy, 'Subclinical neck pain and the effects of cervical manipulation on elbow joint position sense', *Journal of Manipulative and Physiological Therapeutics*, 34, no.2 (2011), pp. 88-97
Joint Position Sense [animation video], created by Dr Heidi Haavik (Haavik Research Limited, n.d.)

people with a low level (subclinical) neck pain and a control group of eighteen healthy and pain-free people. This study tested the brain's ability to determine the exact position of the elbow joint, assessing how the brain uses proprioception (which we discussed previously). The participants in the study were shown how to position their arm when lying down, they were then asked to bring their arm back into this same position when their eyes were closed. They used an electrogoniometer to measure the angle, ensuring accurate results.

The control group, who were healthy and without neck pain, were able to reproduce the correct elbow position consistently. The group with subclinical neck pain, however, were not as good at reproducing the correct position. The study found that when the group with subclinical neck pain were given chiropractic adjustments they were much better at reproducing the correct position for their elbow. The areas of the nervous system responsible for proprioception, which enable the brain to 'see' better were able to function better post chiropractic adjustment, helping the brain to know what was happening in the spine and arms.

As chiropractors we see the benefit of chiropractic adjustments both for the brain and the body. Multiple studies demonstrate further benefits of receiving chiropractic adjustments including improved joint position sense and muscle strength, visual acuity and reaction times. I work with many athletes from amateur to elite and they often come to me believing they have reached a threshold of function and performance. When they receive chiropractic adjustments in the neck and lower back, we see improvement in balance, power, mobility, speed, flexibility and performance. Most of the athletes that I treat find that chiropractic treatment helps them to train harder, get more effective results from training and recover faster from injury. Many of these athletes feel that after receiving chiropractic adjustments they are able to perform on a better level. Each athlete has their own goals. Runners often need help with lower back, hip, knee and ankle injuries and performance, whereas golfers often need help with shoulder, elbow and wrist problems, alongside performance.

In my clinic we help a wide range of patients with many different health needs. Some people want to come off long-term use of pain medication or avoid unnecessary surgery, others want to achieve a physical health goal. Some of my patients in their 80's to 90's also want help with mobility, balance and pain reduction. We have a great collaborative approach with many of the local medical doctors and I view the essential work we do as a pillar of the community.

14 Facts You Did Not Know About Chiropractic

1 Chiropractic, as a profession, has been around for 120 years, but the principles that chiropractic is based on aren't new. In fact the ancient Greeks and other early civilisations used spinal adjustments as a form of healthcare. Hippocrates, the Father of Western Medicine stated that "physical structure is the basis of medicine" and went into great detail concerning the importance of the spine to good health.

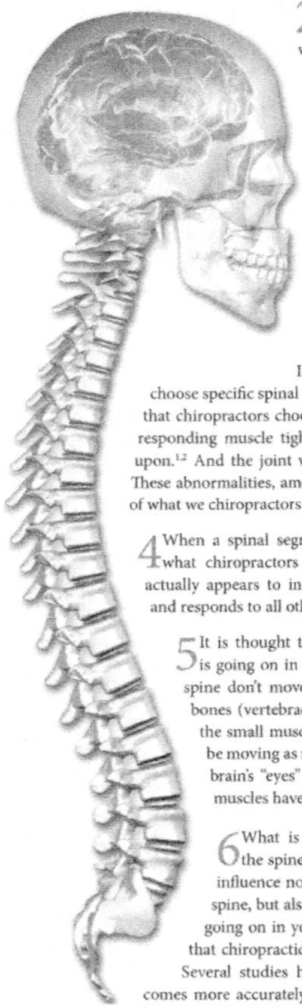

2 There are now approximately 100,000 chiropractors worldwide with over 40 chiropractic schools in 16 countries!

3 Interestingly, chiropractors don't just adjust parts of your spine at random! If you have been to a chiropractor you will have noticed that they touch and feel your spine, move it around, possibly test your muscles to see how strong they are, press on parts of your spine to find out if it is tender at particular points, and so on and so on. In the end they very carefully choose specific spinal segments to adjust. The segments that chiropractors choose to adjust will often have corresponding muscle tightness and tenderness if pushed upon.[1,2] And the joint will have abnormal movement.[3,4] These abnormalities, among others, indicate the presence of what we chiropractors call a vertebral subluxation.[5,6]

4 When a spinal segment doesn't move properly, i.e. what chiropractors call a vertebral subluxation, it actually appears to influence how the brain perceives and responds to all other sensory information.[7]

5 It is thought that your brain cannot see what is going on in the spine when the bones in the spine don't move properly; because if the spinal bones (vertebrae) are not moving properly then the small muscles closest to your spine will not be moving as much, and these muscles are your brain's "eyes" in the spine because these little muscles have loads of movement sensors.[8-11]

6 What is really fascinating is that when the spine is not working properly this can influence not just how the brain controls the spine, but also how the brain can "see" what is going on in your arms and legs. So this means that chiropractic care can make you less clumsy! Several studies have shown that your brain becomes more accurately aware of where your arms and legs are even with your eyes closed![12, 13]

7 So it's a fact that chiropractic care improves spinal function.[14-19] What is really cool is that chiropractic care does not just make your spine work better but it also improves the coordination of your arms and legs![12, 13]

8 12 weeks of chiropractic care even helps you physically feel better! A study showed that three months of chiropractic care improved their participants' physical component of health-related quality of life compared to the control group.[13]

9 12 weeks of chiropractic care has also been shown to improve sensorimotor function related to falls risk in community dwelling older adults. This may well mean that chiropractic care can help to reduce the number of falls that older adults suffer. The results also indicate that the participants themselves experienced a greater physical quality of life after as little as three months of chiropractic care.[13]

10 And to top it off, chiropractic care is safe, even for kids and babies! Chiropractic care for children and infants is rarely associated with adverse events. When they do occur they invariably involve short periods of muscle soreness following an adjustment. Researchers have reviewed all of the published literature relating to chiropractic care for infants and children to see how common adverse events are in our younger patients.[20-22]

11 Chiropractic care has even been shown to help babies with colic cry less! In one randomised controlled trial that investigated the effects of 10 days of chiropractic care on crying time in infants with colic, the babies who received chiropractic care cried significantly less than those who were in the control group.[23] Their crying time reduced by about half, with the babies who received care crying an hour and a half less on average after 10 days compared to the babies that received no care. Multiple other randomised controlled clinical trials have shown that chiropractic manual therapy improves crying behaviour in infants with colic.[24-26] Parents of infants suffering from colic should consider giving chiropractic a go because it could well make a real difference to their baby and their family.

12 Back to the brain, several studies have shown that chiropractic care changes the way your brain sends messages to your muscles![27, 28] So all this research seems to indicate that chiropractic care improves your brain-body communication, helping your brain be more aware of what is going on in the body so it can control your body better.

13 One study has even shown that chiropractic care can make you stronger![29] And the amazing thing is that the changes within the central nervous system seen in this study was very similar to what has previously been shown after 3 weeks of strength training,[30] indicating that chiropractic care has powerful changes to the brain and spinal cord.

14 Recently a study looking at the brain effects of chiropractic found that the big brain changes that do take place when a chiropractor adjusts dysfunctional spinal segments, these changes in the brain take place in a part of the brain called the prefrontal cortex.[31]

By Heidi Haavik PhD

HAAVIK RESEARCH
www.therealitycheck.com

SUMMARY: Power Up

Power Up is the first step to thriving. The Central Nervous System is key to this. It controls every cell, every tissue and every organ in your body - you could call it your Master Control System.

If you don't get your system in S.Y.N.C.™, you could be left with the symptoms associated with physical, emotional, chemical, nutritional and environmental stress. It's important to ask yourself: do you know what causes you stress?

Getting in S.Y.N.C.™ is about listening to your body and understanding what it is telling you. We discussed research on neurology in this chapter, so you'll know a bit more about how your body works and you'll understand the importance of protecting yourself from the devastating effects of stress.

To find out more, so you can continue to power up and support your Central Nervous System with its important function of helping your body to heal and repair, keep reading! In the next section of the book, we'll look at the second step to thriving: working on your body's position.

Getting in S.Y.N.C.™ will help you ignite your Power.

> "The power that makes the body, heals the body
>
> \- B.J. Palmer

PART 2: POSTURE

Keep S.A.F.E. Body Blueprint™

As you'll know from Part 1, your nervous system is central to optimal health. In this section, we're going to look at this in more detail. I'll explain the Keep S.A.F.E. Body Blueprint™, the process I take patients through. This involves working on your **S**tability, **A**lignment, **F**lexibility and **E**ndurance, which all relate to your body's position.

Posture is about your body's position, however usually people think posture simply means being upright; sitting up straight rather than slouching. They don't necessarily think about the posture of their joints and the various factors affecting this. Great posture involves the entire body being in alignment, rather than just being upright. It is about having the strength and flexibility to minimise injury and to reduce the forces of improper alignment that can advance 'ageing' or in other words, wear and tear on the body.

It's important that you understand and action this as soon as possible, even if you're young and healthy. Postural problems, or postural misalignments, don't cause pain initially. They instigate structural changes that lead to a loss of function over a period of time, creating stress on the joints. I always describe it to patients in terms of biomechanics. Basically, if you take an elastic band and load it with weight, it would create what's called stress. If we do that for a period of time it causes a strain, which in physics is known as 'creep'. What happens is that the material will mould and change shape. It's the same with your ligaments. A ligament is the fibrous connective tissue that connects bones to other bones. If your ligaments are put under stress, they will weaken and this damage is called a grade one sprain. If you carry on putting it under stress it will tear, which would be a grade two sprain or even a full rupture.

Everyday activities, such as using a mouse, carrying a bag and sitting down at a desk can place a repetitive strain on your ligaments, causing them to stretch and change shape. The body then responds to that

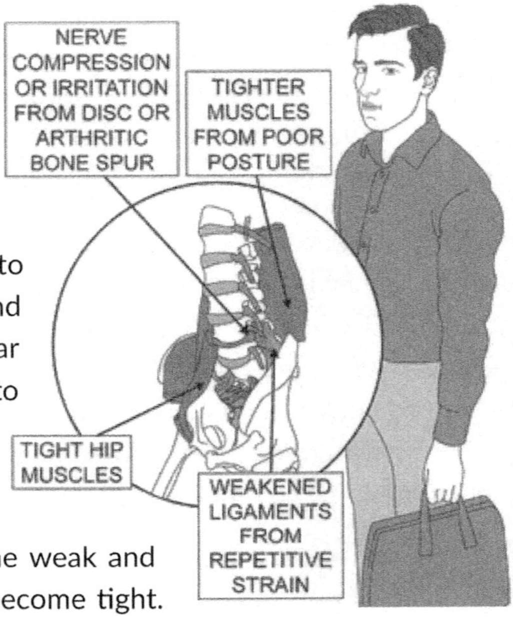

abnormal force and tries to restabilise by fusing the unstable segments. This eventually leads to osteoarthritis where your body creates bone spurs, called osteophytes, to try to anchor that area and fix it. So, with wear and tear over time, your body tries to fuse unstable areas. This causes joints to become stiff because muscles on one side of the joint become weak and muscles on the other side become tight. Once this has happened, it will be much harder for the body to move effectively and over time more health problems will arise from the lack of mobility, the increased pain and if compressing a nerve, arthritis can have serious health consequences.

As mentioned earlier, what we find is that when a joint starts to get restricted, the muscles (which are attached to tendons), become tight and contract thereby pulling on the tendons. This can lead to many things, including pain, irritation and tendonitis. The bottom line is, if tendons get pulled there will be inflammation.

One traditional medical approach is to give a steroid injection, which might help the symptoms by reducing the inflammation, however it won't necessarily treat the cause. As mentioned earlier, physiotherapy or pilates will play an important role on working on strengthening weak muscles and stretching tight muscles, this however is only part of the problem. For the best results there needs to be a chiropractic adjustment as it stimulates the nerves around the joint and we see, in most cases, an immediate softening of the tight area, while the weaker area starts firing up. Working on the tight and weak muscles in conjunction with chiropractic adjustments becomes more effective over time.

People will initially get tendonitis, which will give them pain and affect their ability to do what they want. But over time the tendon can fray, tear or rupture and might require surgery. However, through a combination of adjustments, which won't necessarily focus on the site of the pain itself, we can free up the movement around the joint. Chiropractic care and lifestyle advice addresses the cause, which could be physical, emotional, chemical, nutritional or environmental stress, or a combination of all of them. Identifying the cause and addressing it can help the body to heal and repair itself.

The idea is, that by really understanding what's going on with the body, we can make very specific key adjustments to help realign it. First, we aim to improve stability within the body through the Keep S.A.F.E. Body Blueprint™, a combination of exercise and adjustments. Then, we start to look at alignment through understanding the posture of the body and give a course of exercises to engage the core muscles. Chiropractors don't just look at the muscles supporting the spine; we consider the muscles for every joint in the body and the nervous system which controls the muscles.

These techniques aren't just for those with problems and pain in their body. They provide a really good foundation for general health and will allow you to use your body to its maximum potential. Of course, we have people coming in because they have an injury and they want a rehabilitative process to get well again and get back to what they love doing. We also have people who are in great health, yet they've hit a threshold in ability and they want to take their ability to the next level. If you want to do more advanced sports, for example, working on your core muscles will enable you to play your sports at a higher and safer level.

Once we've got the stability and alignment right, we can start strengthening and conditioning and really build the area up in terms of range of motion and ability. Then, we start looking at flexibility and range, then finally we work on endurance. Let's look at each of these important points in turn.

Stability

Improving stability can help you to maintain long-term health. For example, if someone has an area of instability or a feeling of weakness, as they might describe it, in their lower back, it is likely that the problem will reoccur. As we mentioned earlier in the book, 80% of people will get back pain at some point in their lives and of them around 60% will get a single relapse, 40% will experience multiple relapses and 20% will develop chronic pain. Our goal is to prevent those relapses by teaching people about their body.

Depending on the industry you work in, you may have been taught how to lift items safely to prevent injury during training in manual handling. However, the problem is that this type of training inevitably does not cover all the situations in which you will have to lift something and it often takes place only once every six months to a year, leaving little time for people to really learn. For example, recently I was helping a patient who is a paramedic and has to bend, twist and get into awkward positions to manoeuvre injured people. They're not given core stability exercises in order to help them with these tasks on a daily basis. I also see a number of people who teach manual handling themselves and they often say that they've got their own back problems. Training in manual handling and correct lifting techniques is very important, but that alone is often not enough to prevent back pain.

The role of core stability seems to be quite poorly understood in general. Many of our patients that come into the clinic have been given great exercises at the wrong time, which makes the problem or injured area worse. Core muscles cannot be used as effectively if there is joint dysfunction (misalignment) which often affects the nerve supply to the muscles. Adjusting the spine first resets the signal, thereby allowing muscle activity to be more efficient. This helps people achieve more effective results from their core exercise programme. As discussed earlier, chiropractors call this joint dysfunction and nerve interference a vertebral subluxation.

The type of exercises people need to do will depend on the individual and the nature of their daily routines. We meet each person where they're at and do a full assessment of their lifestyle. Some of my patients will be driving or flying for a living, or working at a desk, several will be more physical, others will be running a busy household and some people will be retired. Everybody's got unique physical, emotional, chemical, environmental and nutritional stresses. A number of people will already have arthritic changes, yet others might have had their very first episode, many people will have multiple relapses and a few people might even be at a point where the body has become hyper-sensitised and have what we call neuropathic or chronic pain.

Once we've carried out an assessment, we will establish an order and sequence for their care. We usually start with adjustments, then work out how we can get them back to their work, sport or lifestyle safely and enable them to get the most out of life on a day-to-day basis.

Scientific research identified by Dr Heidi Haavik has demonstrated that chiropractic care can positively affect many different aspects of health and function. Let's have a look at some of this research in more detail.[10]

A study was conducted which focused on the role of muscle function in stabilising the body and is useful to consider when we look at how chiropractic care can aid everyday mobility. The research subjects consisted of a group of 90 healthy, young students and the study looked at the deep abdominal muscles and their part in the core stabilising system which stabilises the spine and trunk and is particularly important when lifting or moving your arms and legs. In order to stay stable and ensure that the movement in our body is balanced when we lift our arms, we need to 'turn on' these muscles prior to lifting; this process ensures that we can move without injury. This action is pre-planned by our Central Nervous System and happens very quickly, we should not be consciously aware of it. This pre-planned process is called 'feed-forward activation'.

Let us consider our study. In a group of 90 healthy students, 17 of them were unable to pre-activate their abdominal muscles before moving their arms. These students would likely be more prone to injury than their peers who were able to undertake this subconscious process. 13 of these affected students were tested again by researchers six months later and were still unable to activate their abdominal muscles prior to lifting their arms. These students were given chiropractic assessments, these highlighted tightness and restriction in the joints

---

10 Paul Marshall and Bernadette Murphy, 'The effect of sacroiliac joint manipulation on feed-forward activation times of the deep abdominal musculature', *Journal of Manipulative and Physiological Therapeutics*, 29, no.3 (2006), pp.196-202
Feed-Forward Activation [animation video], created by Dr Heidi Haavik (Haavik Research Limited, n.d.)

of their pelvis; the chiropractic term for this restriction and 'nerve interference' is called 'subluxation'.

Each subject was then given a single session of chiropractic adjustments which resulted in almost 40% improvement in their ability to pre-activate their core muscles when they were tested again. I notice a similar improvement on a daily basis when performing muscle tests on my patients, both before and after their chiropractic adjustments. Having this experience backed up by scientific research demonstrates the effectiveness of a chiropractic adjustment on improving muscle-firing activity. After their adjustment, many of my patients feel stronger and able to perform at a higher level of intensity.

In the study, the subjects had not reported any pre-existing pain, however, scientists believe that poor core muscle control may cause pain or injury in the future. I often explain to my patients that if the muscles aren't activating correctly and you have weak core muscles, then when you go to bend or lift, this stress and strain goes into the ligaments. If the muscles are activated, they can protect the spine. By activating the muscles through chiropractic adjustments and subsequently training the muscles with exercises you create a fantastic combination to help people with recovery after an injury. This, in theory, enables the core muscles to activate with the correct firing patterns, thereby protecting the joints and creating stability.

Dr Haavik explains in her work on feed-forward activation:

> "We know from other research studies that people who have low back pain often have delayed activation of their core abdominal muscles when performing various movements. We also know that the brains of many of these people with low back pain are much less aware of what's going on in their lower backs. This means that for many people with low back pain their brains are not receiving or processing accurate information from the small muscles close to their spine, so their brains have to guess what's going on and therefore, may not be controlling the lower back in an ideal way, which can damage the back further. This is why chiropractic care is so important. It can restore proper communication between your brain and your body, so your brain knows accurately what is going on and can control your whole body in the best way possible."
>
> - Dr Heidi Haavik

Let's use the knee as an example. The knee is made up of bones, the meniscus, which is the shock absorber and ligaments that stabilise the joint. The ligaments are basically straps that stretch around the bones and hold them in place.

When you bend to lift something up, the ligaments mould and change shape, especially if the muscles aren't supporting the spine properly. If that continues over time, the ligaments can tear or rupture.

When there has been a repetitive sprain or strain for long periods of time, often it's not healing because partly, somebody has not changed their lifestyle that's causing the stress on the area, also sometimes the body is responding in a way that is increasing this stress, fatiguing the area and causing further damage. So, by working on that we can help the body stabilise, so it heals naturally.

Take the example of Pete, a lift engineer who had back problems:

> "I can't function without a strong back and I do a lot of crawling and things that normal people don't do. When you get older you probably need a bit of maintenance that you didn't when you were younger - it's just common sense. I was very sceptical at first. I couldn't see how small movements and changes would make a big difference. The changes are so gradual that you don't really think anything's happening. But then when you sit back and reflect on it, you realise that you've made huge strides in your life and you can lead a normal life again without worry, which I credit to coming here."

When Pete came to our clinic, I gave him a specific diagnosis. From understanding what was going on in his lower back, I then gave him the appropriate chiropractic adjustments and suggested the correct exercises to do in the gym to support it. On top of that, we worked together on his mindset. The combination of all three really helped him. Chiropractors see many patients who are sceptical initially, especially if they've had a treatment before that hasn't necessarily worked for them and they're being told different information by their doctors. However, it is great to hear from patients such as Pete, who are able to function better in their work and daily life after treatment with us. My goal is to focus on helping people to sustain good health in the long-term, rather than treating symptoms in isolation.

Alignment

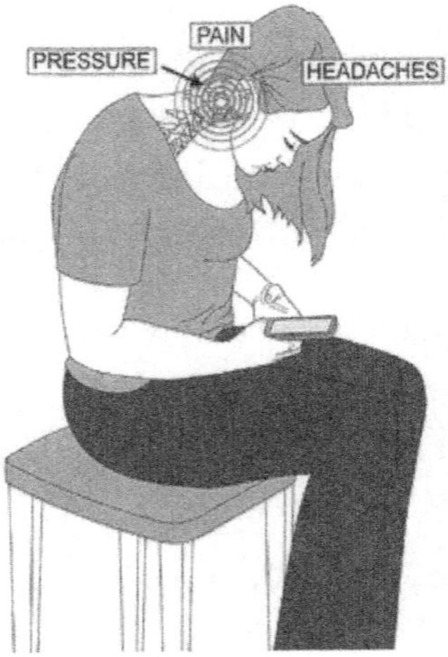

Alignment is closely related to posture. When we look at posture for the spine, we look at the position of the head in relation to the neck and the shoulders. Much of the time, people get into what we call Anterior Head Carriage, which means that the head comes forward. This happens as a result of, in many cases, looking down to read, looking down at our computers or potentially from stress or depression.

This type of posture flattens the curve of the cervical spine, which places strain on the joints and restricts the range of movement in the neck. Over time, this causes an imbalance in the flexor and extensor muscles of the chest and upper back, a condition that is sometimes referred to as Upper-Crossed Syndrome. This is characterised by a weakening of the rhomboid (upper back), neck flexor (front of neck) and lower trapezius muscles, while the pectoral (chest) muscle, upper trapezius (back of shoulder) muscles, suboccipital muscles and the sternocleidomastoid muscle, (the muscles in the side of your neck, known as SCM for short) become tight. Over time, these muscular changes cause the shoulders to roll forward and head to drop forward. This can cause pain in the neck or headaches and can lead to early arthritic changes. Some people might even develop a disc injury, because the head is equivalent to the weight of a bowling ball, so if it's being loaded in that position, over time it can have that effect on the ligaments we mentioned earlier.

If the shoulders rotate internally, which could be caused by many everyday activities such as carrying a bag, typing, using a mouse, sleeping on your shoulder, or even carrying a baby, there will be pressure on your tendons, which can lead to tendonitis.

So, when any joint is under stress for a period of time, you get wear and tear. This usually happens in those areas of the spine that are under most load, which causes the spinal curve to change. Where this happens will depend on someone's lifestyle – for example, if they're over-training a particular part of their body in the gym or if they have a very sedentary lifestyle – as well as whether somebody has had a specific injury, such as whiplash. The spine is supposed to have a normal natural curve and what happens is that people lose core stability and the head comes forward.

Modern lifestyle habits can contribute to this. When we check our mobile phone, for example, we're effectively training ourselves to look down, which can change the curve of the neck quite dramatically. As a result, we're seeing more and more patients, younger patients, with neck pain than we ever used to. Smartphone users can help to prevent injury by holding their phone higher up, using a headset, or using the voice function to dictate what they're writing rather than looking down and typing it in. It's not about stopping using your smart phone, it's just a case of being more mindful of how you're using it and trying to maintain good posture. Basically, it's all about habit and breaking bad ones that are causing wear and tear on your body.

Research implicates the loss of the curve in the cervical spine, known as loss of lordosis or, in worse conditions, cervical kyphosis (a reversal of the curve) as accelerating the degeneration of discs and joints in the spine. Potentially even causing inflammation and irritation to the spinal cord, which may ultimately lead to tethering or demyelination.

This can lead to autonomic problems, including affecting areas that control breathing and hormone release.[11]

Poor posture can lead to Upper Crossed Syndrome, which can cause wear and tear in the neck and lead to pain. A seated position can cause muscular imbalances in the lower part of your body. This is referred to as Lower Cross Syndrome, which people can develop by simply doing their job. You might work at a desk all day, meaning that you're spending prolonged periods of time sitting down. It's the same with driving long distances. Prolonged sitting can lead to shortened iliopsoas (muscles in your inner hip) and one of the hip flexor muscles, which leads to tightened lower back muscles, weakened abdominal and core muscles along with weakened gluteal muscles. This weakening of the core and glutes causes more stress on the lower back, making you move in an altered pattern. This increases risk of injury and pain.

Helping people with these postural imbalances first involves assessing the movement of their joints and spine. Then, we focus on freeing up movement by stretching those muscles that are tight and strengthening the muscles that are weak, through adjustments initially and then later through exercises. These exercises are similar to what someone would do in a pilates class or what they might do with a physiotherapist. The problem is that if you've got an injury, stretching a tight muscle might irritate the joint that's injured, so there's a time and a place to do that and that's where you need a professional who really understands your body and will know when an exercise may aggravate and when an exercise will help. We always advise people

---

11 Augustus A. White and Manohar M. Panjabi, *Clinical Biomechanics of the Spine*, Second Edition (n.pl: Lippincott, 1990)
Alf Breig, *Adverse Mechanical Tension in the Central Nervous System*, (n.pl: Almqvist and Wiksell, 1978)
PC Wing et al., 'Back Pain and Spinal Changes in Microgravity', *The Orthopedic Clinics of North America*, 22, no.2 (1991) pp.255-262
Kentaro Shimizu et al., 'Spinal Kyphosis Causes Demyelination and Neuronal Loss in the Spinal Cord: A New Model of Kyphotic Deformity', *Spine*, 30, no.21 (2005) pp.2388-2392

to listen to their body and if an exercise hurts, then stop doing it and get reassessed. The 'no pain, no gain' mentality is for training healthy muscles, this is not the same mentality needed for rehabilitation.

Chiropractors assess what's called the kinematic chain. This is a concept in engineering that's useful for describing movement in the human body. Imagine a simple chain. It is a series of connected links and movement in one part of it affects movement in another part. Similarly, in your body, movement in one area affects movement in another, because the different parts of your body all connect. If somebody has a problem in their shoulder, elbow, or wrist and are displaying symptoms in, say, a weakness in grip, they could actually have a problem with their neck that's triggering it.

A chiropractor would assess the whole chain. If a runner is getting problems with their ankle, for example, I would assess the ankle as well as the muscles at the knee, hip and spine and how the nerves interact with the joint. We're looking at how the alignment of the body can have an impact on movement. This is particularly important if you love walking or running. If you've got a slight misalignment, over many miles, the body is going to have to compensate for it, which can eventually lead to injury.

B.J. Palmer, the Developer of Chiropractic described this process whereby small movements can lead to injury perfectly in his 'big idea'. He said:

A slip on the snowy sidewalk in winter is a small thing. It happens to millions.

A fall from a ladder in the summer is a small thing. That also happens to millions.

The slip or fall produces a subluxation. The subluxation is a small thing.

The subluxation produces pressure on a nerve. That pressure is a small thing.

The pressure cuts off (or interferes with), as we now know, the flow of mental impulses. That decreased flowing is a small thing.

That decreased flowing produces a dis-eased body and brain. That is a big thing to that man.

Multiply that sick man by a thousand, and you control the physical and mental welfare of a city.

Multiply that man by a million, and you shape the physical and mental destiny of the state.

Multiply that man by one hundred and thirty million and you forecast and can prophesy the physical and mental state of the nation.

Now comes the man. Any one man is a small thing.

This man gives an adjustment. The adjustment is a small thing.

The adjustment replaces the subluxation. That is a small thing.

The adjusted subluxation releases pressure upon the nerves. That is a small thing.

> The released pressure restores health to a man. That is a big thing to that man.
>
> Multiply that well man by a thousand, and you step up the physical and mental welfare of a city.
>
> Multiply that well man by a million, and you increase the efficiency of the state.
>
> Multiply that well man by one hundred and thirty million and you've produced a healthy, wealthy, and better race for posterity.
>
> So, the adjustment of the subluxation to release pressure upon nerves, to restore mental impulse flow, to restore health, is big enough to rebuild the thoughts and actions of the world.
>
> The idea that knows cause, that can correct the cause of disease, is one of the biggest ideas known. Without it, nations fall; with it, nations rise.
>
> This idea is the biggest I know of.
>
> - B.J. Palmer
> The Developer of Chiropractic

In a nutshell, correcting subluxations improves your life force, or your power, by restoring effective communication between the brain, your nervous system and the rest of your body. This enables you to feel as healthy as possible and function at your best in everyday life.

When I'm talking to my patients, I use the well-known golf analogy to explain the compounding effects of the 5 Dimensions of Stress. This example is used in the financial industry to explain compound interest, I use it here to illustrate the compound effect of stress. Individually, each stress in our life may be minor, however the compound effect of these stresses can lead to devastating results for our health.

If you were playing a round of golf for 18 holes and I suggested betting one pound on the first hole and doubling it thereafter, one pound becomes two, two becomes four, four becomes eight etc. It doubles each time and by the time you hit 18, it's £131,000. If you went just three more holes it would go to over one million pounds, such is the drastic compound effect of stress on our health.

HOLE 1	£1
HOLE 2	£2
HOLE 3	£4
HOLE 4	£8
HOLE 5	£16
HOLE 6	£32
HOLE 7	£64
HOLE 8	£128
HOLE 9	£256
HOLE 10	£512
HOLE 11	£1,024
HOLE 12	£2,048
HOLE 13	£4,096
HOLE 14	£8,192
HOLE 15	£16,384
HOLE 16	£32,768
HOLE 17	£65,536
HOLE 18	£131,072
HOLE 19	£262,144
HOLE 20	£524,288
HOLE 21	£1,048,576

Three more holes would generate

That same effect of repetitive physical, emotional, nutritional, environmental and chemical stresses over time has a compound effect on your health. The question is, are you depleting your health from your choices that you make, or are you increasing it? It all comes down to choice. As Dr James Chestnut says, most chronic health conditions that are lifestyle induced could be termed "suicide by lifestyle."

There's always going to be an example of someone who smoked 100 cigarettes a day and lived a long life. We all know that cigarettes are bad for us and we know that poor posture and high levels of sugar and stress are also bad for us. Unfortunately, most people put off changing their lifestyle.

Very few people actually take action from other people's experiences. It's only when they start to go into crisis mode that some people begin to take action and even then, not everyone takes action and even if they do, it's not always the right action. Unless people make changing their health a high priority (a MUST) the results they want are going to be hard to achieve.

If you haven't found the right professional, find somebody who gets this concept, who understands it, who wants to help you. Find someone whose message, understanding and technique resonates with you and find someone who you can trust to get you well. My advice to you would be, if you have had injuries and traumas in the past where you've had a fracture or you've had stiffness or restriction, get it checked and you'll know how your body is functioning. There might be things that you could do to improve your core stability, posture and alignment, which would help you with your ability to do the things you love to do, whether that's horse riding, walking, playing golf, going to the gym, work, or in some cases, having a family.

Take Anna's story as an example. Anna was diagnosed with Symphysis Pubis Dysfunction (SPD) during her pregnancy. SPD is a condition that occurs when the joint at the front of the pelvis (the symphysis pubis) is not working as it should be. Together with the two large joints at the back of the pelvis (the sacroiliac, or SI joints), the symphysis pubis plays an important part in holding the pelvis steady during any activity. If the joint is not firmly 'tied' by its ligaments it cannot perform its role effectively, resulting in excessive strain being placed on all the pelvic joints. The pregnancy hormone 'relaxin' softens and 'relaxes' the ligaments of the body to allow the pelvis to open slightly during labour in order to help the baby move more easily through the pelvic canal. It is important to remember that as the hormones of pregnancy equally affect the sacroiliac joints, they too become slightly looser. It is, therefore, common for the problem to exist with one or both of the sacroiliac joints, with this putting extra stress on the symphysis pubis.

"I was diagnosed with Symphysis Pubis Dysfunction (SPD) when I was 13 or 14 weeks pregnant, but I'd been feeling pain from about 8 weeks. I went to the doctors, but they thought it was just normal pregnancy aches and pains. When it got to 14 weeks, the doctors realised that it wasn't just ordinary aches and pains, but they couldn't offer me anything that worked. I went through their physio, had hydrotherapy pool sessions booked on the NHS, but they kept cancelling them because the pool was closed. I even got booked onto a 'pain workshop' where I had to sit on a hard chair and was told that pain was all in the mind. I had to imagine my pain was a bee flying away, which obviously did nothing about my actual pain!

At 17 weeks, I was on crutches. They offered to induce me early, but I didn't want to do that. I ended up having an emergency C-section, but my SPD hurt even more than that. Post birth I got prescribed painkillers, which I didn't really want to take because I was breastfeeding. At mother and baby groups, I struggled to get up off the floor after we'd been sitting down. It hurt even to breathe, I always tried to take shallow breaths. The doctors kept telling me that it would just go away. So, when I met you at the Chislehurst Summer Fair, I thought I'd see what you could offer me. In our first appointment, you explained what you could do. After a month of regular visits, the pain began to lift, which was amazing. When I fell pregnant again, by which time I had a two-year-old, a job and two dogs, everyone told me that the SPD pain would come back and would probably be even worse than before. But, after my treatments with you, I was pain-free throughout the pregnancy. Now, I've got no problem getting up and down at mother and baby groups."

In Anna's case, the gentle adjustments helped to recruit the stabilising muscles in the pelvis and Anna reported feeling more comfortable, in fact her back felt stronger and better aligned after each adjustment.

Flexibility

Flexibility is not only about being supple. It is the ability to turn, bend, flex, move, any joints in the body freely. The correct balance of muscles means that you're not too stiff and not too flexible, so your joints can work in their normal range, not a reduced range or hyper mobile range.

Often if we get someone to turn left and right, they can't turn as well in one direction as the other because there's reduced range of motion. It's the same with your shoulder; one side might not move as well. Rather than just accept it, you might be able to have better range of motion to relieve pain and improve your function on a daily basis.

By function I mean strength and fluidity of movement – it's about you being able to do what you want to in life, because you're able to move not only in a pain-free range, but in a normal range for those joints. Normal sounds boring, but actually it's about allowing the joints to perform at the best they can. Obviously, certain sports people such as gymnasts or martial artists can increase that flexibility, giving their joints a different range of motion, but anyone can gauge whether their flexibility is in a normal range or not by considering their posture: how you turn and bend, but also how you get up and go for a walk. Do you have tight muscles? Do they fatigue quickly? Are they functioning properly? If you have a tight muscle, it can lead to inflammation over time, as I mentioned earlier.

A lack of flexibility can lead you to pull or tear a muscle. If the muscles overlying a joint are tight, the joint will rub more and this could lead to wear and tear. It is important to have normal flexibility around all joints in the body and for all joints to be well lubricated, allowing them to move in a healthy way.

It has been demonstrated with clinical research that when the upper three neck vertebrae become stiff and restricted through the use of a collar this creates abnormal mechanoreceptor (pressure receptor) signals in the nerves, leading to a reduced dexterity. In other words, lack of movement affects the nerve supply and signals that created over time can lead to reduced flexibility, increased adhesions and changes in co-ordination. The current approach, where possible, is to get mobility back. The use of supports can be beneficial, when necessary, however should not be a first resort as it leaves a longer-term challenge with rehabilitation.

Other than chiropractic adjustments to create flexibility there are some fantastic exercises that you can supplement your care with that stimulate the joints neurology for both range of motion and core control. The neck muscles are also linked to the eye muscles. Looking left to right and up and down and to each corner without moving your head a few times can release the neck muscles and improve your range of movement. (Please check with your chiropractor or health professional before trying a new exercise).

One of the ways we assess flexibility as a chiropractor is when we palpate or examine the spine; this is known as joint-play. If an area is not moving properly, it is considered loss of joint-play and this restricted motion segment has a lack of segmental flexibility. Say if you love walking, yet your hip flexors and back muscles are tight because you've been sitting all day, when you go for a long walk, because the forces aren't normal, your spine could potentially rub and cause irritation and discomfort and if it rubs over a long period of time you can increase the wear pattern. Some people lose the flexibility, they can't even put their shoes or their socks on.

A great exercise for increasing flexibility of the hip flexors is a glute bridge exercise, however if the muscles are very weak and/or you have other injuries, the position of this exercise can lead to cramp in the hamstrings, or it can lock up the segment in the spine which can pinch tissue or get irritated. As always, it's about meeting somebody where they're at, assessing them and giving specific adjustments according to their needs. Always keep in mind, any new exercises are best prescribed and checked by a knowledgeable practitioner.

Endurance

Endurance means different things to different people. For an athlete, it's the ability to do more. For some people, it's how long their adjustments are going to hold and how quickly they can get back to life: how long can I walk for before my back hurts, or how long can I do whatever activity I love to do?

Building endurance is about strengthening the body over time. You're going to retrain the body and change habits that might be causing a problem. Endurance increases gradually as your body heals and strengthens.

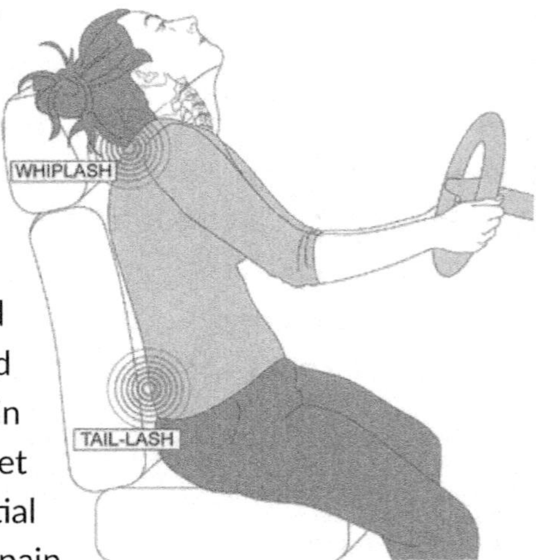

I had a patient who had a car accident that caused neck pain, headaches, left arm pain and lower back pain. She had been in pain for seven months before being referred to my clinic by her GP. Painkillers had stopped being effective and the exercises had not helped, in fact the pain had seemed to get progressively worse. Our initial adjustments helped reduce the pain significantly. One of the changes that helped build endurance was to use a lumbar cushion at work. Her poor posture was not causing pain before the accident, however once the spine had become injured in the accident her poor posture was slowing recovery down. In her case a cushion helped decrease spinal stresses and in turn help speed recovery and increase endurance.

Once the changes were made, she noticed the endurance in her body's ability to work improved and her body healed.

Of course, fitness comes into it, but there's a difference between aerobic fitness and spine or joint fitness. For example, when people talk about increasing their fitness levels to go from couch to 5K, or 5K to 10K, or even to run a marathon they're generally talking about aerobic fitness. Spine fitness or joint fitness is about being able to do activities in daily living without re-injuring. It's allowing your body to do whatever you'd like to be able to do, whether that's lifting weights, going to the gym, playing with the kids. Whatever it is in your life that's important to you. If you've lost the ability to do that or you're worried that you might lose the ability to do that because of the injuries you've had, it's about reaching a certain level of strength and spine or joint fitness to do what you want. It's a moving target because, as you get better, you can do more and improve it over time.

Some people have lacked mobility for so long they no longer believe they can improve. There are patients that might come in and say, "I've tried this exercise. I've tried seeing another therapist. Things didn't work for whatever reason." It's a bit like weight loss. Sometimes people will say, "I've tried every diet". When you actually ask them, they've maybe only tried three or four, but they didn't necessarily work on their mindset first. It's not that they've failed. It's not that the diet failed. It's not that whatever they did didn't work. It's that order and sequence of events did not work for that particular person, at that particular point in time.

In order to create lasting change your body needs endurance. The starting point for achieving this comes from motivation.

Motivation is just the spark to get people going, it's actually consistency that people need in order to improve. Say somebody wants to lose weight and one of their main methods for losing weight is to get fit by walking. Unfortunately, they then injure their knee and walking causes pain and potentially could cause a long-term knee problem. They could still lose weight by working on their nutrition and there's many other exercises they can do that wouldn't affect the knee, so they could still exercise.

For some people though, what happens is they think 'that's my thing, I'm going to walk', then when they can't walk because of an injury, they lose their momentum and that breaks their motivation. In clinic I see many patients who have a health goal of losing weight, yet they have a set back from a back or a knee injury that inhibits their ability to do that. We can address their problems with their back and knee and work with them to increase their strength and in the meantime, they can still work on other approaches to weight loss, whether it's mindset, nutrition, or doing other types of exercise. As the endurance in the knee increases over time then getting back to walking is indeed possible.

We encourage people to challenge any limiting beliefs they may have that they are restricted. Of course, there are cases where people might have health conditions that really make it very difficult however, it doesn't mean that it can't be done. It's working with an expert who really knows the body, who can make sure that whatever they're doing is safe for that person and working at the pace that's right for their body. Some people might have a heart condition. Others might have a back problem, or even have had a surgical procedure. It's doing the right thing at the right time and having professional support to guide them through that process.

There are certain misconceptions around endurance. For example, sometimes people misjudge their level of endurance when recovering from an injury. They use pain as a guide, instead of how their body is functioning and understandably think that everything is fine once their pain has gone away, so they get back to their usual activities and often suffer a relapse. It's not that the problem has gone away and come back. It's that the underlying problem didn't go away in the first place. Approximately only 10% of the brain detects pain, so pain, or lack of pain, is not a good indicator of healthy function.

I see this with clients who are really committed to certain types of sports. They are really keen to get back to it as soon as possible after an injury and sometimes go back a little too early. Chiropractors will aim to get people back to their sport as quickly and as safely as possible, which may mean doing different types of exercises to what the client is used to. We'll find the right balance so people can keep a level of fitness while still allowing time for rehabilitation. Endurance is about maintaining a certain level of fitness so that when people are able to then go back to their activity, their body will heal better.

Whether working with a professional athlete or someone who needs to get back to manual work, there are real demands on time and pressure to get someone back to health as quickly as possible. Sometimes because of this, it's a fine balance and getting the right advice will inevitably speed up the recovery.

Endurance might mean that your back does not keep going into spasm or 'go out' when you complete normal activities of daily living such as making the bed or carrying shopping bags. For some of my patients however, endurance means having the ability to run a one-hundred-mile event or cycle two-hundred miles.

When you're thinking about endurance, ask yourself what your goals are: what are you trying to achieve? Sometimes people do a particular type of exercise just because other people do it, or they've been advised to do it, or they think it's the right exercise to do. For example, if you go to the gym, you don't necessarily need to do dead lifts, or high intensity interval training (HIIT), which is an increasingly popular form of exercise promoted by the fitness industry. Dead lifts, by nature, aren't necessarily a great exercise for the spine, so unless you're competing, or doing something that involves you needing to do dead lifts, it's not necessarily an exercise I'd recommend for spinal fitness. Similarly, while HIIT can give you a range of fantastic benefits, it can also lead to shoulder and back injuries. It's about doing the right exercise for you, which I believe comes down to understanding what's important for you and your goals. With the right professional support, you can identify the best form of exercise for you.

SUMMARY: Posture

Your body's posture is fundamental to its health. Maintaining good posture and movement will prevent injury and help to give you the energy you need to THRIVE. You can work on your posture through the Keep S.A.F.E. Body Blueprint™:

Stability means listening to your body and addressing areas of weakness. I'd strongly encourage you to get assessed by a chiropractor to help identify areas you need to strengthen and you can do so much for your health by doing gentle/specific exercises for your core.

Alignment is essential for preventing injury. It's about maintaining the right posture to enable your body to move efficiently and safely.

Flexibility is important for balancing out everyday movements that can cause strain and areas of tightness in the body.

Endurance is about strengthening and conditioning your body, by maintaining your stability, alignment and flexibility for long-term health.

So, how can you get the motivation you need to keep S.A.F.E.™? It's easy, once you've found your purpose, which we'll discuss in the next section of this book.

PART 3:
PURPOSE

Mind Mastery Matrix®

Purpose is about finding your WHY. Tapping into your inner driving force, giving you resolve, resilience and conviction. It's the compelling reason why you do anything. If we're under any level of stress, we go into fight-or-flight mode. When we are in this mode, our body starts to kick out adrenaline and cortisol, which are the neurotransmitters and hormones that are related to the stress response. That makes our heart rate go up, increasing our blood pressure and creating an increased sensitivity to pain. Our digestion gets inhibited, as it's no longer a priority for the body. We also don't need our immune system, so that gets inhibited. We don't need our memory, so we start to get brain fog. When this has been going on for some time, people start to become ill. Stress is one of the leading causes for chronic health problems and death in the western world.

As mentioned in the 5 Dimensions of Stress chapter, fight-or-flight is a normal response to a stressful situation. It helped early humans to survive when, for example, they were at a watering hole and a tiger jumped out at them. What's not normal for our bodies is the stressful situations that we end up in through work or our personal lives, giving us a constant, chronic low-level of stress. Our body is not designed to stay in this state for extended periods of time. Sometimes, we get this response before anything has even happened. This is created by our thoughts or stress about a particular event or situation, rather than the event itself.

For example, if I ask people, especially older people if they like snow, I usually get a few grumbles. Maybe one or two people like the snow however, the large majority of people don't. Their perception is that they are going to be stuck inside, unable to get out. They're worried about losing their independence and having a slip or fall. So, the meaning that they give the snow creates the feelings they have. A stress response can be created as a result of this. Whereas, when I ask children if they like the snow, usually hands shoot up and they can't wait to get outside and play in it. Therefore, the meaning that we give an event in our life can really dictate our emotional response to it, which leads to the entire physiological response as a result.

I would like to share a defining moment from my life that changed the course of things:

It was October 2006 and I was catching up with my friend Steve from Liverpool. We were doing some karate training and he gave me a gift. He gave me a Tony Robbins CD called 'Get The Edge'. After listening to it, I realised what I needed to work on. I wouldn't be able to make a difference or be able help others if I kept going back into a state of procrastination. Some of the biggest challenges people need to overcome are the mental blockers that stop them from taking action.

This was the catalyst that launched my journey into personal development. On the way I discovered that so many people are suffering and there is so much that can be done to help. That's when I decided that my life's purpose is to create change and help as many people as I can. That purpose has led me to develop skills that I didn't even know I needed and create change in my local community. It's a journey, not a destination. I do not have all the answers, what I do have is a passion and drive to make a difference.

Tapping into my purpose is my fuel to facilitate change. I see so many people suffering unnecessarily and so much can be done to help which is why I made it my life's purpose and mission.

This part of the book is about purpose: how to find it and change it if you need to. Although we can't always change the events that happen in our lives, we can change the meaning we attach to them. This then alters our physiological experience, which impacts on our health. You can do this by working through the eight different steps in this section: Mindfulness, Meditation, Music, Memory, Motivation, Mantras, Momentum, Musts.

Mindfulness

Mindfulness can have significant health benefits, reducing stresses and helping you to focus and be present in the moment. Mindfulness practice can be undertaken as part of your daily routine and involves simply learning to appreciate how even the simplest of living beings are utterly complex and to take in the beauty of the world around you through the power of your senses. It's about maintaining an awareness of your thoughts, feelings, sensations and surrounding environment and accepting yourself and your situation without judgement. It is about being present and living in the **NOW**, not the yesterday or tomorrow. It helps you to engage with your purpose by enabling you to deal with the mental tensions that result from the stresses and strains of everyday life. It is a quality or state of being conscious or aware of something.

Crucially, mindfulness gives you choice. Anger or guilt are examples of emotions from our past, whereas fear or anxiety are emotions about our future. These thoughts are pictures, images, feelings and maybe even distortions of reality. Through managing your state of being, you can learn to change your mindset, to help you learn to let go of the past and future and focus on the now.

In the past chapter, we learned about the importance of posture for good health. You might not expect to read about posture in a section on mindfulness, but they relate in important ways. Allow me to highlight some of Dr Heidi Haavik's work into the key area of posture. When a person has bad posture, they may get neck pain or headaches and someone who suffers from neck pain can often have problems with their breathing. How we breathe influences our posture, our spinal stabilisation and can impact our daily functional ability and life. You might be interested to know however, that poor posture can also affect other aspects of your life.

For example, Dr Haavik highlights a 2015 study conducted at the University of Auckland, New Zealand. This study took young healthy people and looked at the effects of upright and slouched posture on their ability to cope with a stressful reading task. The study showed that when the people had an upright posture, they could cope with the task far better than those in a slouched position who were doing the same task. It was also reported that people with a good upright posture felt that they had a higher sense of self-esteem, a better mood and a lower level of fear compared to those with a slouched posture. So, good, upright posture does not only affect our bodies and our breathing, it can also help with self-confidence, happiness, stress and fear, thereby potentially making a person more resilient when dealing with stresses. [12]

Have you changed your posture as a consequence of reading this? If so, when becoming mindful about your posture you probably noticed that it was not what you wanted it to be.

Try this exercise. Sit in a slumped posture with your head down, eyes down and say the phrase in a low tone: "I am happy, I am happy." Now sit up straight, bring your head up slightly above neutral, smile and say: "I am sad, I am sad." For most people they feel low in the first example even though they are saying, "I am happy" and feel energised

---

12 Shwetha Nair et al., 'Do slumped and upright postures affect stress responses? A randomized trial', *Health Psychology*, 34, no.6 (2015) pp.632-641
Chiropractic & Posture [animation video], created by Dr Heidi Haavik (Haavik Research Limited, n.d.)

in the second. This shows that posture, tone and focus have an impact on how we feel.

Did you do this exercise, or did you just read through the words? This is a great example of mindfulness. If you didn't, please take the time and a brief moment to pause, re-centre yourself and do the exercise now.

If you are mindful with how you hold yourself, taking care to adopt an upright position and maintain good posture it will not only help with your physical health, it will also potentially impact on your mental and emotional health. This in turn helps you to be more mindful, since it helps you to breathe properly and appreciate the world around you. Posture and mindfulness are linked in a positive behavioural cycle, connecting your physical, emotional and mental health.

Mindfulness is an easy way to lower stress levels and reduce the risk of its effects, such as high blood pressure and a weak immune system. Practising mindfulness once a day can significantly reduce these dangers and lead to a better quality of life. It can also help you to focus and improve your memory, making it easier to reach your health, business or lifestyle goals. Studies have shown that when you are mindful about eating, you consume less food than when you are not, which can have a massive impact on the body's health over time. The mind-gut connection. Our thoughts regulate the balance of hormones that allow us to digest our food. Watching T.V. or being in a state of fight-or-flight can inhibit digestion or even affect the body's ability to recognise when over-eating has occurred.

Being present is so important. How frustrating is it when you go out for a meal and friends or family are checking their phones rather than having a full and present conversation?

So, what daily activities could you undertake to practise mindfulness?

I would encourage you to mindfully read the rest of the book, thinking about how the advice here can positively impact your health. It's easy to read a page and have your mind wander.

Mindfulness Exercises:

1. Mindful posture:
   - Notice your posture
   - Bring your neck and head up in a relaxed way
   - Relax your shoulders back
   - Notice if your spine is straight
2. Mindful eating:
   - Relax
   - Eat slowly
   - Taste every mouthful
   - Notice the texture, the smell, the taste
   - Think about your body digesting the food, the nutrients released. Is the food healthy?
3. Mindful gratitude:
   - Create a list of 21 things you are grateful for
   - Then focus on each one, see what you saw or feel what you felt. Get a deep sense of gratitude
4. Mindful exercise:
   - Take the core stability exercise such as glute bridge, or wall stretch and notice where there needs to be a tweak in posture, tension, breathing
5. Mindful relaxation:
   - Sitting or lying down

- Notice the muscles in your jaw relax
- Now notice the muscles in your neck and shoulders soften
- Now go through every muscle in the rest of your body, from head to toe, scanning and sending focus, followed by a deep relaxing breath to the muscle

Meditation

Mindfulness and Meditation are interlinking practices that teach methods to help you switch off from the pressures and demands of everyday life. They can calm your overactive brain and nervous system and stimulate the 'rest and digest' part of your body.

Meditation is a simple yet powerful technique that connects the body, thoughts and breath and can enable you to live in a more mindful way. As people feel increasingly overwhelmed by the pace of modern life, it's no surprise that there has been a surge in the popularity of meditation in the western world in recent years.

You might think that meditation is simply about relaxing, however it's much more than that. It involves focusing on one thing, whether that's a single image, object, sound or breathing pattern in order to make you fully present in the moment, with an enhanced awareness of how your body and mind feel. For much of the time in life, we're running on autopilot - we'll learn more about this later on in the book when we think about habits. There's so much that we do without thinking about it. The whole time, our brains are processing so much information – the sights, sounds and smells that we encounter when we're running around at work or at home from phones, televisions, computers, traffic or other people. Think of the mind like a computer. If it keeps on going and going, never hibernating or shutting down, then sooner or later it's likely to crash.

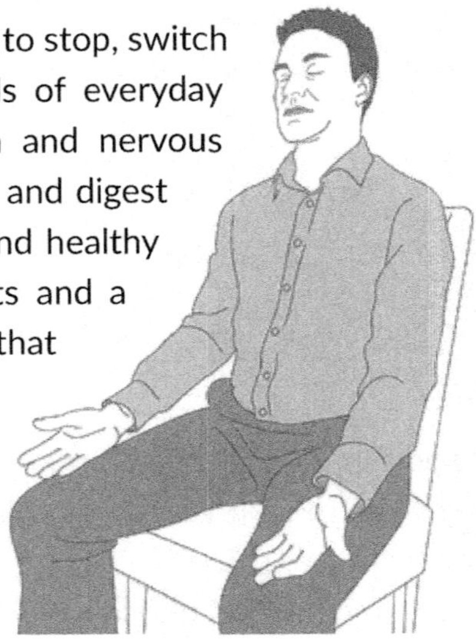

Meditation gives you the opportunity to stop, switch off from the pressures and demands of everyday life and calm your overactive brain and nervous system in order to stimulate the rest and digest part to your body. It is a drug-free and healthy alternative to taking anti-depressants and a stand-alone or complementary route that we would recommend to any patient suffering from pain that may be a result of emotional strain. (Please don't stop taking any prescription medication without consulting with your doctor).

Often people say, "I can't meditate" or "I've tried it, but my mind keeps wandering." Think of it like exercise, it becomes less of an effort over time. As you practice and train the brain it becomes easier.

Do you take the time to meditate, even for only a few minutes a day? If not, what could you do, or change to build that new habit?

Music

What's your favourite song? Maybe you don't have one favourite song, maybe you have a few favourites that you listen to at particular times, such as classical music when you want to relax at home or something more upbeat when you start doing exercise. Think about the last film that made you cry, frightened you or made you think. In films, your emotions are largely created or enhanced by music. It makes you create a story in your mind, affecting how you perceive your situation in the present.

The fact that music can affect your mood tells you that it can have a strong influence on your brain and body. It can actually increase or reduce your heart rate depending on the genre. Music can be an important part of an overall holistic treatment programme. It has the capacity to reduce feelings of stress, helping you to work on building a positive mindset. The right type of music can induce feelings of calm, making you feel peaceful, uplifted and inspired.

Research has found that our brains and bodies will sync to the frequencies around us. Dr Kaplan's research on neuro-acoustic harmonics looks at how different tunes and frequencies can be used to improve memory, concentration and focus.

Music is a useful component for some of the treatment programmes that I recommend for my patients. We use it with a device called BrainTap, which is a simple, relaxing way to re-balance your brain during your day. BrainTap is an innovative system used to deliver Self Mastery Technology (SMT). This transformational technology combines gentle pulses of light and sound with visualisation and soothing music to return you to the right balance of brain wave activity. A simple twenty-minute session produces the relaxation response, a state known for reversing the damaging effects of stress, reducing worry, anxiety and providing the same benefits as 3-4 hours sleep.

Whilst most brain training programmes use games and puzzles that take conscious effort, SMT utilises the BrainTap headset that lets you relax and listen to empowering mind messaging audio sessions. These are strategically encoded with neuro-sensory algorithms for the most productive power nap imaginable.

Regular use of SMT, by reducing the effects of the stress response, stimulates healthy brain chemistry, boosts energy and the immune system, promotes weight loss, purges unwanted habits, installs new behaviours and can dramatically improve your quality of life.

You remember our lift engineer Pete, he also used BrainTap to great effect as part of his treatment:

> "The treatment here has changed my life and it wasn't just the adjustments. We also talked about mindset. It's a stressful world we live in anyway and I now do meditation to cope with all the stress I deal with. The BrainTap sessions fill you with more hope and lift you. They affect you quite deeply, you can feel a direct influence from the mind set tapes. The physical exercise I do three times a week down in the gym, the BrainTap and coming to your clinic for treatments are probably the three most important things that I do in my life now. I feel quite tearful just talking about it. You don't realise it until someone says to you, 'tell me about yourself. Tell me what you're going through.' Then by talking about it, you can see it more clearly."

To find out more about BrainTap, please visit the online resources section at www.5tothrive.co.uk for more information and a complimentary trial.

SCAN ME

Music can be a powerful health tool. If you're mindful of the music you listen to on a daily basis, you can use it to tap into your purpose and practise mindfulness. If you're interested in exploring this further and finding out how the BrainTap device can help you, please visit our clinic or alternatively all the information you need is in the online resources section that accompanies this book.

Certain music you might listen to could make you feel sad, angry or excited. Be conscious about the emotions that you would like to experience and check to see if the music you listen to is supporting you to achieve your goals.

Memory

We learnt about memory in the earlier chapter on neurology, *remember*? Memory loss is often associated with Alzheimer's or dementia. However, what is also very common is memory impairment, which can happen as a result of stress. When we exist on autopilot, our brain loses functional neurological capacity and long-term stress could be a precursor to deterioration of brain function. Stress hormones interfere with our brain activity and pathways and in turn affect our capacity to be really 'switched on'.

We discussed before how your spine and muscles can affect the way your brain works and 'sees' the world around you and chiropractic research continues to demonstrate how the function of the spine can influence the brain. Dr Heidi Haavik, highlights a 2016 study in a hospital in Denmark[13]. The study involved a group of people who had never had any chiropractic care before. The study was split into two sessions, a session where the participants received real chiropractic care and a session where the participants received pretend (also known as sham) chiropractic care, this is similar to a using a placebo group in drug trials.

Both of these sessions used an electroencephalography (EEG) to record whole-head brain waves using 64 individual electrodes. The results showed that after a chiropractic session there were clear changes in the way the brain functioned, while after the sham chiropractic session no such changes were recorded. A brain function change of an average of almost 20% was recorded after the chiropractic session.

---

13 Dina Lelic et al., 'Manipulation of Dysfunctional Spinal Joints Affects Sensorimotor Integration in the Prefrontal Cortex: A Brain Source Localization Study', *Neural Plasticity*, 2016, ID 3704964 (2016) 9 pages
Chiropractic and the Prefrontal Cortex [animation video], created by Dr Heidi Haavik (Haavik Research Limited, n.d.)

By using electrodes across the whole head, it was possible to observe where in the brain the changes were happening after the chiropractic treatment. The researchers observed that the changes were most likely taking place in the prefrontal cortex. The prefrontal cortex sits at the front part of the pre-frontal lobe of the brain. Dr Heidi Haavik describes it in her work, 'Chiropractic and the Pre-frontal Cortex' as follows[14]:

> "This part of your brain is a little bit like the conductor of the brain, making all the other parts of your brain cooperate together in perfect harmony. The prefrontal cortex is the area of the brain where your executive functions take place. This means it is very important for our everyday behaviour. It's the part of the brain needed to be able to carry out all goal-directed tasks, decision making, memory and attention, intelligence, processing of pain and emotional responses to it, autonomic function, movement control, eye movements and spatial awareness."

These changes to the prefrontal cortex from receiving chiropractic adjustments may explain some of the changes we commonly see within chiropractic care, such as improved muscle and motor function and even an improvement in memory. The 2016 study was conducted and analysed by non-chiropractic scientists which is very important as it shows there is no doubt that adjusting your spine changes the way your brain functions.

You can train your memory through particular exercises, just as you can change your body. Memory exercises are an easy and simple way to improve your memory and sharpen your mind. The first and most

---

14 Ibid.

important thing is being present. Being present in the moment can help you focus on tasks and when practised, it can help prevent your mind from wandering and improve your mindfulness. Experiencing stress makes you less likely to remember things and keeping in the moment can help reduce the risk of memory impairment. Learning how to control and release stress is a really powerful way of letting go of anxiety and worry.

The second most important thing is to stimulate the five senses. Memories relating to an event are scattered across the brain's sensory centres. If one of the senses is stimulated to evoke a memory, other memories featuring other senses are also triggered. Utilising these different exercises uses the phenomenon of neural plasticity that literally revives your brain's neurons, building up a bank of memory circuits. There are so many fun ways to do this, such as listening to new music, taking up art, tasting new food, learning how to do massage. Doing new activities creates a reservoir of new neurons which can enable you to remember and learn new things. You could even take up dancing, start a new exercise programme, play Sudoku, or simply make an effort to take a different route to work or learn a new language. This stops you from functioning on autopilot and challenges your brain.

Modern research in neuroscience has challenged the traditional view that the brain is fixed and that over our lifetimes we gradually lose nerve cells, known as neurons, which gradually causes a decline in brain function. In the book 'Super Brain', Deepak Chopra and his co-author, Prof. Rudolf Tanzi of Harvard Medical School explain that it is possible for us to improve our brains. The brain regenerates and renews itself every day and the experiences we have on a day-to-day basis can form new neural pathways in our brains; this is known as neuroplasticity.

What we experience day-to-day can be seen as input for your brain and we can consider actions and thoughts as an output. This creates what is described in neuroscience as a 'feedback loop'. Anything we experience using our senses is a neurological input for the brain and if it is a new experience then your brain is learning something new and creating new neural pathways.

As 'Super Brain' describes it, the more positive the input, the better your brain will function. A Buddhist monk meditating on compassion, for example, will develop the brain circuitry that brings compassion into reality. Depending on the input it receives, you can create a compassionate brain, an artistic brain, a wise brain, or any other kind. If input shapes the brain, then happiness and well-being are created by giving the brain positive input. This is about much more than just positive thinking. It includes a range of things and activities, such as having good friends, sustaining a lifelong companionship with a spouse or partner, engaging socially in worthwhile projects, finding and following your purpose in life and leaving time for play and relaxation.[15]

This is similar to using creative visualisation for success. For example, if you have a fear of speaking you can meditate on being a successful speaker and the act of visualising this can rewire your brain to achieve this, as happened for me. Sportspeople too, can visualise their race, golf swing or fight for example, and achieve success with those things in the physical world. We can rewire our brains by changing the input, by creating the thoughts, feeling, actions and eventually results we want. To improve our grey matter, we have the ability to increase our functional neurological capacity through training our brain.

---

15 Deepak Chopra and Rudolph E. Tanzi, *Super Brain: Unleashing the Explosive Power of Your Mind to Maximize Health, Happiness, and Spiritual Well-Being* (n.pl: Harmony, 2013)

What things can you do that will help you improve your memory, thereby creating new neurons? Anything from spatial awareness exercises, music, touch, hearing and new experiences can help you develop your memory.

Motivation

Motivation is the spark that creates the driving force for change. You're not going to train your brain or body without the motivation to do so. So how do we get motivation, where does it come from? Motivation comes from having a purpose, emotionally compelling reasons why we get up every day.

It is important to live with a meaningful purpose. Often, we go out of our way for other people, more than we would for ourselves. Having a strong sense of purpose or a reason to do something will motivate you much more to achieve your goals. Motivation can also help you to stop habits, such as smoking or drinking. Some people find they do more for others than they do for themselves.

A serious health challenge, such as having a heart attack or getting an injury, can be a very powerful motivating force. However, that might not work for everyone. If you've gotten used to living in a particular way, such as being a heavy smoker, even knowing from stacks of evidence that you'll suffer for it in the long term might not be enough to motivate you. Instead, if you know deep down you really need to change and are struggling with finding the motivation it might be that you need to change your focus point.

In my Mind Mastery Matrix® workshop, we dive into these areas to help people identify their motivating forces.

What do you think it takes Sir Mo Farah to get to the point he's at? Do you think he sometimes feels like having a duvet day, or eating fast food? I am sure he does, just like the rest of us! What makes him carry on? We all have the potential to be motivated on a daily basis, we just need to work out what our WHY is.

It's so easy to use softeners in our language: "It's okay." "I'll do it later." "I'll try." I think to myself, Why Just Survive When You Were Born To THRIVE?

What motivates you? I had the privilege to meet Keith Cunningham, one of Tony Robbins' gurus in Fiji and something he said to me really struck a chord. He said, "hell on earth would be to get to the end of your life and meet the man or woman that you could've been." Just imagine it. Imagine meeting the person you could have been. How much better would your life be if you could learn to master your stress? Developing an awareness of your WHY and what's holding you back is the first step towards finding your motivation. Once we've done that, we need to start conditioning it with language.

List 3 unresourceful habits that you would like to break.

E.g.

1. Procrastinating
2. Smoking
3. Poor Posture

1. ______________________________
2. ______________________________
3. ______________________________

Mantras

So, what are mantras? Mantras are the words and phrases that we use when talking to and about ourselves. They are said in a positive way in the present tense, such as: 'I *am* focused', 'I am *healthy*', 'I *am* happy', 'I am *energy*', 'I *am* love', 'I am *motivated* and achieve my goals', 'I *am* action orientated, I *get stuff done*'. Also play with changing where you place the emphasis when you say these mantras out loud. The focus and attention on different words that you choose to emphasise will feel different and have a powerful effect to help train your subconscious mind to assist you.

The power of the words we use and the emotions behind them literally shape our world. The challenge is that sometimes the language patterns can have a negative impact. This can affect your self-esteem, confidence, happiness and quality of the relationships in your life. Some examples of negative patterns are:

- I can't
- I don't know how
- What if they don't like it?
- I'm not good enough
- What will people think if...

This generally stems from the fear of not being enough or being rejected. If we use phrases like this, it can prevent us taking the action we need to. The limitation is not the lack of a skill, it is the thought process we have.

Our beliefs create our reality and our language expresses our beliefs. For instance, people who are busy and working hard might come home to their family tired and burnt out. If, however, they have the mantra, 'I'm going to give my family the best of me, not what's left of me', are they likely to show up differently and be more present with their time when they are there?

The language and thought patterns that we have can help us to achieve greatness or create limitations and glass ceilings. Repeating positive and empowering phrases can help us tap into our brains neuroplasticity and literally rewire our brain for success.

Limiting beliefs strongly affect your outcomes in life because they can drive what you do, or don't do. It's amazing what you can achieve and what you can get out of life on a daily basis, if you really put your mind to it.

Let's consider the inspirational life story of Nicholas Vujicic. Nick was born Australia in 1982 without arms and legs. Many of us would struggle to envisage what life would be like under these circumstances. Nick's website, Life Without Limbs, paints a picture:

"Imagine getting through your busy day without hands or legs. Picture your life without the ability to walk, care for your basic needs, or even embrace those you love."

We might find it hard to believe that a person would be able to live their life as fully as others. Yet, Nick refused to allow his physical condition to limit his lifestyle. Throughout his early life Nick struggled with depression, loneliness and the challenge of being 'different' to the other children and he questioned both the purpose of life and if he had a purpose of his own. Nick found his strength and passion for life through his religious faith and his family, friends and other people who have inspired him throughout his life. He is now a successful public speaker, husband and father, who has travelled around the world, sharing his story with millions. He lives a full and varied life as an author, musician and actor with hobbies including fishing, painting and swimming.[16]

I heard Nick speaking at a seminar and found his story incredibly inspiring. It shows that anybody can live a life without limits. Mantras are a powerful way of challenging your limiting beliefs and creating new, empowering beliefs that will help you to THRIVE.

If you believe that you can't do something, or you can't achieve something, you are much less likely to. Sometimes your mantras and limiting beliefs can become a self-fulfilling prophecy. Think about the difference, for example, between somebody saying, "I'm perfect for this job, this is the perfect job for me." They send out a CV and they don't hear anything versus somebody with low self-esteem who says, "I'm not going to get the job. I'm going to send the CV anyway."

The person with the negative outlook is not likely to pick up the phone and find out whether they got the job or not. If they haven't heard anything, their answer is, "well, obviously it wasn't meant to be." Whereas on the flip side, if they go, "this is the perfect job" and they've not heard anything, they'll pick up the phone in a confident way, in a confident tone and say, "I was just ringing to check, did you get my CV?" That positivity on the phone might be the thing to make someone say, "oh, this person sounds interesting. Let's invite them in," or it might get them useful feedback that they can use when applying for another job.

Think about what events, situations and circumstances cause you stress. It'll be different for everybody, depending on your personality.

---

16 Nick is President of the international non-profit ministry, *Life Without Limbs*, established in 2005 Nicholas Vujicic, Bio, n.d. <http://www.lifewithoutlimbs.org/about-nick/bio/>

We all have people in our lives that could be described as 'mood hoovers', 'energy vampires' or a 'fun sponge' - the people who seem to take more than they give and make you feel drained of energy. Sometimes, we can even be that person to ourselves.

However, you can use language in a positive way to help you feel motivated, energetic and vibrant by creating mantras. Once you've done the 'I am' mantras, write affirmations: 'I laugh every day', 'I am loved' 'I am confident', 'I am healthy'. You can say them out loud, or silently, as long as you still do it with energy and passion. Just saying the words on their own doesn't work. You have to feel the emotion behind it for your brain to make the important changes that we have discussed. Saying 'I know' can change your beliefs and convictions. 'I know I am healthy, I know I am healthy'. It might feel strange doing this at first, however when you step out of your comfort zone and try something like this, you initiate changes in your physiology and brain which really starts to change how you feel and behave.

Saying 'I am healthy' or 'every day, in every way I am getting healthier and healthier', will help train your mind and it's highly likely you will find yourself making healthier decisions. It's really important when you use your mantras to have an energy and feeling behind it. For example, if you use a mantra 'I am grateful', pause and picture the things you are actually grateful for.

Our brains filter what we see and experience, so you can shape your reality by changing what you say to yourself about it. It doesn't get rid of whatever was causing stress, but it changes our state. It gives us choice, allowing us to be resourceful rather than defensive.

By replacing words such as '*try*', '*should*' or '*need*' with powerful phrases that inspire, you can change your thoughts and actions, which will ultimately change your results. When creating your own mantra always make sure to use the present tense and be positive. Please avoid using negative language such as "I don't want" in a mantra. For example, if you say, "I don't want to smoke" the subconscious part of the brain only hears 'smoke'. Instead you could say, "I will only breathe clean air today!"

What are your 'I am' and 'I will' mantras for each day?

Complete the following mantras 'I am... I will...' with empowering statements such as:

'I am... happy, grateful'

'I will... do anything I set my mind to'

'I can... eat healthy food every day'

'I believe... I can do this'

'I know... I have the resourcefulness'

'I must... enjoy the journey'

Use these words in your own mantras: am, will, can, believe, know, must.

I am... ____

I will... ____

I can... ____

I believe... ______________________________________

I know... _______________________________________

I must... _______________________________________

Momentum

Once you've found your motivation and worked on your mantras, you need to work on making it happen. You need to build momentum.

It takes effort to make a change. If you think about a playground roundabout, it takes exertion and energy to get it moving round. It needs a big first push, then a few more, then, once it's gathered momentum, it only needs a tap to keep it going round.

So how can you build momentum? It takes perseverance - just long enough until you start seeing the change, then it becomes easier to sustain it, to keep the roundabout turning. It only takes one degree of change to get things moving.

What's the one thing you need to do to make a difference, to start a change? It might be something that you've learnt so far in this book. If you can take one thing you can do today, start doing it and keep at it, you'll gather momentum. It's not about changing your entire life in one go; it just takes one shift. Think about something you could change now and imagine what your life will be like a year from now if you keep doing it. It could be spending more time with your family, going for a run a couple of evenings a week, volunteering one morning a week, committing to reading a certain number of pages of a book each week. It could be buying a journal and writing in it, using the positive language of 'I will', 'I know'.

There are so many simple things you can do, starting now. If you've started to exercise before or you have been on diets to lose weight, but have not succeeded, don't beat yourself up about it. You may have been trying to change too much all in one go. Consider maybe swapping one unhealthy snack for a healthy one or watching just half an hour less television each evening and doing some basic exercise or stretches in your front room. Once you've made that first change, you create momentum and that carries you forward, making future decisions about how to live an optimum life easier and easier.

To give a personal example, many years ago I started training in karate. When I first started training, there were so many times that I felt too tired and drained to go to the Dojo. I made that initial push and now, I'm a black belt in karate. I didn't even think about not going to training. Once I'd gathered momentum, it was so much easier to keep moving forwards.

So much time is wasted during daily life which could be utilised. Once you cut down on wasted hours, for example watching television or scrolling through your phone, you'll have more time. Even if it's only half an hour, the possibilities are endless. Taking this time to do something productive or to practise mindfulness will greatly improve your quality of life. The small subtle shifts in your day, over time, will gradually better your lifestyle.

> You have the energy to do more, how will you use it?

Musts

The final step is musts. Do you ever think, 'I should do that', I should do this'? If you *should* do something, you don't *have* to do it and it's all too easy to end up not doing it. Then you blame yourself and feel bad about it. When you turn it into a must though, you get that conviction. You'll prioritise it and commit to it - and that's what gets results. By changing 'shoulds' to 'musts', you'll be better able to focus on the things you can do that will radically improve your quality of life.

Musts are a critical component to create your success. Whether it's to break an unresourceful habit or make a difficult change, often you will need to stop something or start something. If you want to lose weight you know you should eat more healthy foods and less or no unhealthy foods. You should exercise to a certain level of intensity and have consistency. By changing the word 'should' to 'must' and having a commitment to make progress, your chances of success go up exponentially.

So, what must you do?

Consider these questions:

How are you going to be more mindful? How will you create space and time for mindfulness in your home and your daily routine?

What about your music? What type of music will you start to listen to?

What about meditation? When will you learn how to do it and what type of meditation works best for you?

What one new thing will you start to learn to help with your memory?

What mantras are you going to start saying?

What's your motivation, your WHY, your spark?

What's going to be different when you've finished reading this book?

What must you do?

Give yourself some time to think about these questions and make up your own. Then focus on your one degree of change: the one thing you're going to do to change in order to gather momentum. It's not about giving yourself yet another to do list: it's about focusing on what you must do, choosing to do it and committing to the choice.

A question that you could ask yourself every morning is: what can I do today to improve my health and why is it important?

Having an accountability partner, coach, mentor or peer group can really help you make faster progress as your verbal or written commitments of 'musts' helps you to focus and stay on track.

SUMMARY: Purpose

I advise my patients to adopt the Mind Mastery Matrix®, using the 8 M's: Mindfulness, Meditation, Music, Memory, Motivation, Mantras, Momentum and Musts. Incorporating these into your life on a daily basis will help you to feel inspired and motivated: it will enable you to reconnect with your purpose.

Why not try writing down three things that, if you do them, will change the course of your health? Is it to eat healthy food, to give up food that will harm you? Or is it to take up meditation, mindfulness, or even book a BrainTap session?

Remember, we always have choices over the meanings we attach to events in our life and the attitudes we hold.

> "It's not the events in our lives that shape us, but beliefs as to what those events mean."
>
> - Tony Robbins.

PART 4: PERFORMANCE

Fuel to Thrive®

Once you've worked on your Power, your Posture and your Purpose, it's time to put it into action, through your Performance. By Performance, I mean how you act and feel in your daily life. In this part of the book we're going to learn about how you can get that vibrancy, that spring in your step to enable you to perform and fire on all cylinders. As you'll know from the first part of this book, being holistic is about listening to your body and finding solutions, not only to get you out of pain but also to help you to live your life to the fullest on a daily basis.

Our body relies on what we eat, the fuel we put into it, in order to function. However, the relationship between food and health sometimes gets obscured. People are fed by the food industry, which generally pays no attention to health and are treated by the health industry, which generally pays no attention to food. It's not that medical professionals don't want to, it's just that many doctors aren't necessarily trained in nutrition properly, so they don't always have the resources to be able to help you. Nutrition can have a profound effect on your health. However, to feel this effect you don't have to do a dramatic overhaul of your diet all in one go. As we learnt in the last chapter, change happens little by little. In terms of changes you can make for your health, there are few things more fundamental than taking steps to give your body the fuel it needs to THRIVE.

Symptoms

Your body uses what you eat to build and repair muscle tissues and make new cells, which contributes to how your body works on a daily basis: how you move, sleep, fight off illness, through to dealing with pain. It therefore makes sense to look at what fuel you're putting into your body. Are you helping it, or are you hindering it? Is what you're eating going to make new healthy cells or unhealthy cells and is a body with unhealthy cells going to have more or less symptoms?

When it comes to diagnosing and treating people who are feeling unwell, medicine tends to look at symptom control and relief, whereas a holistic or a natural approach examines why you're getting that symptom in the first place. There are two reasons why our body might be imbalanced with food. Either you are putting too many of the wrong things in, such as toxins, chemicals, pesticides and additives, or you're not getting enough of the core nutrients that you actually need to be able to work properly.

When something has not been working in your body for a while, or you're doing things that aren't good for you, it puts your body into a state of dis-ease (where your body is not working at its best). If your body has been working in a state of dis-ease long enough, it can become a disease process. Diseases don't come out of nowhere. Usually they're the result of a long-term chronic build-up of the state of dis-ease throughout your body.

It's true that we have genes related to certain health conditions. However, one thing that dictates whether a gene actually becomes a problem is our environment: our stress levels, what we eat and what toxins we're exposed to. We have more control over our gene expression than we think. This is the field of epigenetics, the study of how environment changes gene expression.

First, it's important to understand your symptoms. It's easy to misread your body and end up giving it the wrong fuel. If you're feeling lethargic for example, always have a mid-afternoon slump or get out of bed feeling tired and going from one task to another feeling bored or feeling a lack of energy, it's easy to feel that you need sugar for energy. However, we know that sugar is damaging to your health. Sugar is very addictive for the brain, so why do you think companies put sugar in all their processed foods? It makes things addictive and gives you cravings for more, whereas in reality, our body requires healthy fats, which are the real energy source we need. Our body mistakes this need for healthy fats as a craving for sugar.

When it comes to nutrition there are many conflicting opinions and theories. To help you with this, here is a simple way to think:

> If you can't kill it or pick it, don't eat it.
>
> Or if you are a vegetarian or a vegan:
>
> If you can't pick it, don't eat it.

Basically, processing food puts chemicals and additives in and this, ultimately, is not healthy. These chemicals are synthetic and therefore potentially toxic to our system, sometimes even acting as neurotoxins.

Sugar, like many other processed foods, is very acidic. For our body to work at its best, we actually have to be slightly alkaline. To be specific, our blood needs to be at a pH level of 7.36. Acid is 0-7 and alkaline is 7-14. The challenge with acidity is that our body finds it very difficult to work in an acidic environment and it reduces the oxygenation of your cells quite drastically. Too much acidity causes a significant amount of inflammation in the body. Cancer cells grow and flourish in an acidic environment[17] along with fungus, bacteria and viruses. This clinical research has observed that if someone gets very sick,

17 Yasumasa Kato et al., 'Acidic extracellular microenvironment and cancer', *Cancer Cell International*, 13, no.1 (2013) p.89

the acidity could actually be used as a marker for cancer and further research has shown that cancer cells create an acidic environment to enable them to grow and metastasise.[18]

One current nutritional viewpoint is that a number of chronic health problems are an acidity problem that has developed over time. Acidity and alkalinity could also have impact on losing weight, because if we're a bit more acidic, our body holds on to more fat to act like a buffer against the acidity. This might be why some people find it so difficult to get rid of that last little bit of fat, even if they're doing exercise. Their body could be holding on to it to try to protect itself against the acidity. Also this viewpoint goes on to suggest that when you're acidic it's also harder for you to absorb nutrients, because the inside of your gut forms a very thin lining to protect it from getting damaged which makes it harder for you to absorb your nutrients through the gut wall. This could explain why some people are deficient even though they may be eating healthy food.

When you have increased acidity in the blood, the electrical charge changes around your red blood cells making them clump together. As a result, less oxygen can bind to them, so it reduces your oxygenation. This could be why we can feel really tired and run down with low energy. We just haven't got enough available oxygen. Acidosis is caused by either an overproduction of acid that builds up in the blood or an excessive loss of bicarbonate from the blood (metabolic acidosis) or by a build-up of carbon dioxide in the blood that results from poor lung function or depressed breathing.

---

18 Nazanin Rohani et al., 'Acidification of tumor at stromal boundaries drives transcriptome alterations associated with aggressive phenotypes', *Cancer Research*, 79, no.8 (2019) pp.1952-1966

The following symptoms could be signs of acidosis:

> Tiredness, dry skin, brittle nails, fatigue, poor digestion, muscle weakness, cold hands and feet, headaches, sleepiness, confusion, seizures, diarrhoea, increased heart rate and shortness of breath.

Acidosis is the medical condition; however, the nutritional theory is that small changes in acidity can lead to subtle symptoms putting the body in a state of dis-ease. So, while sugar and other processed foods might give you a temporary boost of energy and make you feel better, they will be harmful in the long-term and make you feel even more tired.

As well as too much acidity, too many toxins can cause tiredness. Our liver is our filtration system and sometimes it has too many toxins to filter at a time, causing a back-up and congestion. It's important to give your body the chance to cleanse. This doesn't necessarily mean going on an extreme diet for seven days where you only drink hot water and lemon. It is just about concentrating on putting lots of goodness back into your body. Water is definitely an important part of it, but there are many different ways of cleansing your body and giving it the fuel it needs to really THRIVE. We're going to go into this in a more detail in the next sections.

Nutritional Mindset

Every decision you've made on what to eat, every decision on how much exercise to do, will inevitably be reflected in your health. So, your health in the future is going to be a reflection of decisions you make today to change and move forward.

I'm sure you've heard the phrase, "you are what you eat?" As cliché as it sounds, it's very true. As mentioned earlier, "the food that you eat can either be the greatest form of medicine or the slowest form of poison." Whatever your body consumes it will process and can ultimately affect your energy or performance. For that reason, it's important to think about food as fuel. It can heal your body and enable you to harness your body's natural energy source.

As well as what you eat, your overall mindset and how you think about food are very important. As we learnt earlier in the book, stress produces adrenaline and cortisol. These hormones in themselves can make you more acidic, which, as we just discussed, makes it difficult for your gut to absorb nutrients. So, if you eat when you're stressed, you're not actually going to absorb all the goodness from your food.

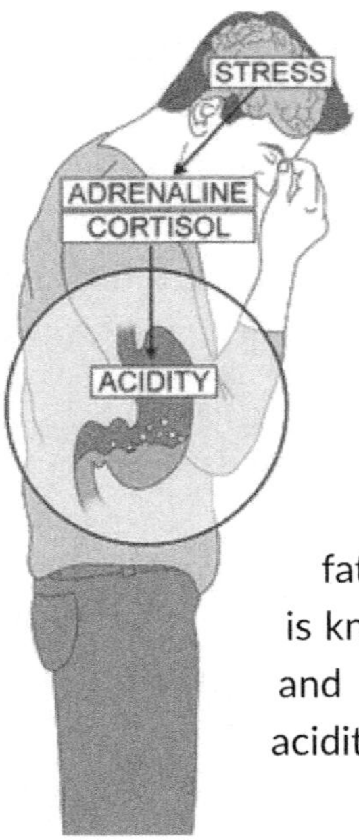

Additionally, when we have pain and inflammation, we create prostaglandins and fatty acids, this inflammatory process creates what is known as an inflammatory soup, these hormones and neurotransmitters involved also increase our acidity.

I'm sure you've heard people talk about the health benefits of the Mediterranean Diet. It contains lots of fresh fish, healthy fats such as olive oil and fresh fruits and vegetables. Another reason is that they take their time to enjoy their food. They have family time where they eat together and food is an important part of their social and cultural life. When you are stressed and rushed you cannot digest your food properly. Having a relaxed and enjoyable fresh and healthy meal is really important for your health. Unfortunately, in today's society many people live by a 'grab-and-go' lifestyle and guzzle down a quick sandwich or lunch on the way somewhere.

Just because food is fuel it doesn't mean it has to be boring! There are so many delicious, healthy foods out there, it's just a case of experimenting to see which ones you like the most. Trying new things will help you to break out of bad eating habits. Someone once said to me, if you're not hungry enough to eat an apple, you're probably not hungry at all. You're probably bored or it's a habit. We eat for so many reasons, however we should primarily be eating to fuel our bodies. If you feel hungry, try having a drink of water first, because often the first sign of dehydration is hunger. Ask yourself whether you are you actually truly hungry, or if you are just picking for the sake of it.

One of the first simple habits you can change is how you walk around the supermarket and what you put in your trolley in the first place. Try challenging yourself to do most of your shop by just going down the aisles that have fresh food. Don't even go down the biscuits, cans, meats, dairies, or frozen aisles. If you don't have it in your trolley, you won't have it in your cupboard.

A modern lifestyle makes it much harder to stay healthy than it was a generation ago because there are many more chemicals now, we exercise much less and tend to have more desk-based jobs. There's so much more against us, so we have to make that bit more effort to stay healthy. It's very hard to get it absolutely right, unless you have your own allotment and grow everything yourself out in the countryside where there's less pollution. The key is to make the effort and not get stressed about it. Just do your best and follow the 'compared to what' philosophy: look at your options and weigh up which one is better for your body with what you have available at that moment.

It's really helpful to be mindful of what you're eating. Have you ever found yourself sitting in front of the T.V. with a bag of crisps or biscuits and the next thing you know it's all gone? Remember, if you feel hungry, ask yourself this: "am I hungry enough to eat an apple?" If you're not, you're probably not that hungry at all! You're probably bored, or maybe you're feeling emotional and want comfort food. Maybe you're anxious and that's sending mixed messages to your body, making it feel like it needs fuel when really, it doesn't. If you keep going back to the fridge, opening and closing it and not seeing anything you want, again, you're probably not really hungry. Try having a drink of water first then see how you feel after 20 minutes or so.

Our body is mostly made up of water and often we don't drink enough of it. If our muscles don't get enough water, they get stiffer. If our joints don't have enough water, there's less lubrication. Our organs struggle to function efficiently and our body cannot cleanse properly if we don't have enough water. You'll be surprised what a difference just drinking water can make. So, thinking about the composition of our body and acting on it by drinking water as well as eating good food, is key to developing a strong nutritional mindset.

How To THRIVE

Your liver, digestive system and bloodstream all need to be able to function efficiently for you to THRIVE and they are directly affected by the food you choose to eat.

Your bloodstream carries oxygen and other key nutrients to the cells in your body. The individual cells also make up our organs, so if we have healthy cells, we get healthy organs. Our body is constantly regenerating. For example, blood cells live for 120 days. So, if one cell has a 120-day lifespan and you start eating good healthy food, which starts making healthy cells, over time you can actually have brand new blood! The main things cells need are oxygen, water, nutrients and the ability to get rid of waste products. You can help your cells to do this and regenerate efficiently by rebalancing your acidity and making your body more alkaline. The body has an innate inbuilt mechanism to balance itself called homeostasis, however by abusing your system over time it will struggle to adapt. This is why being kind to your body and nourishing it will allow the body to heal and repair itself more effectively. Providing your body with a rest from chemicals and additives that it isn't designed to digest makes sense.

Sometimes though, when you start eating healthily, you actually begin to feel worse. That's because many of the toxins we put into our body are stored in fat. As the fat starts to break down when you begin eating healthily and exercising, the toxins are released back into your body.

That's why you can sometimes feel worse before you feel better, however if you continue, in many cases your body will start to improve. It's the same when people stop caffeine. They can get headaches and feel tired. This can also happen generally with our body in losing weight. It's just because we're eliminating many more of the stored toxins that have built up in our body.

According to Tony Robbins – there are seven main principles to detoxification:

Cleanse and re-build your liver and colon

Superhydrate

Develop a healthy nutrition plan

Regularly lymphasise

Perform low impact exercise

Build a strong immune system

Ensure your body has the ability to rebuild itself

It's really interesting, many of the current popular trends in healthy eating have many areas in common and make similar recommendations as to what is good for us to eat. The Alkaline Diet for example states that certain foods create an alkaline by-product when digested and metabolized. Lemons, for example, are said to be extremely alkalizing after digestion and this has been observed to make urine output more alkaline. Fresh lemon water and apple cider vinegar are recommended in The Alkaline Diet as alkalising and dark, leafy green vegetables are also considered very alkalizing and highly nutritious.

There are many things you can do to stimulate your lymphatic system (which is like the body's drainage system) and energise your body, this is often referred to as lymphasising. Gentle stretching and exercising, such as rebounding (jumping on a small trampoline), really helps to get lymph moving. Dry body brushing, in an upwards motion towards the heart also stimulates the lymphatic system, as does massage. Breathing deeply is also really important. Use your diaphragm to take a really deep, long breath. Put your hands on the side of your ribs and feel them flare out- your chest shouldn't move much, it should all be coming from the lower part of your body. Yoga and pilates are also helpful for your breathing as well as getting you moving and stretching.

Exercise is really good for you, as most people know. However, too much intense exercise can cause a build-up of lactic acid and inflammation, this can lead to 'overtraining flu'. So, it's about getting the right balance. As you're just starting to increase your exercise, if you do too much without balancing yourself, it can make you more acidic. So, if you're just starting out, the guide that you need to go by is the breath test. If you're exercising aerobically you should still be able to easily have a conversation. Build up your exercise slowly.

Exercise and food go hand-in-hand. Sometimes people think that if they exercise, they can eat what they want, however that's not the case. Your body is a system, it's completely connected and what you do in one area of your body, such as what you feed yourself, affects what you can do in another area, such as how far you can walk or run. You need your nutrition to correlate with the exercise you're doing. If you have a goal to run a marathon or build muscle for example the nutritional requirement would be different. Protein is an essential key for a healthy and balanced diet and you can get protein from fish and meats as well as legumes and nuts.

Prebiotics and probiotics are also really important for helping you to feel well and energetic. It's all about getting good gut bacteria. This will help your digestion, which is fundamental to your ability to absorb nutrients from your food.

Do we really need supplements?

There are some very good quality supplements out there as well as cheaper low-quality products. Most nutritional therapists that I have interviewed assess their clients' individual needs.

The current school of thought seems to be:

1. Supplements should not be used to replace a balanced diet
2. If you take supplements you should still aim to have a healthy diet
3. Inadequate amounts of vitamins and minerals can lead to health problems
4. Some vitamins and minerals are unsafe at high levels
5. Some supplements can interfere with medication – if you are unsure you should check with your nutritionist or doctor. (For example, patients on warfarin should be careful with fish oils as it can affect your INR)
6. Nutrients can be lost from poor diet, poor food storage, poor food preparation and low-quality foods
7. Some health conditions make it hard to obtain or assimilate the nutrients your body needs
8. It is much harder today for people to get all their vitamins and minerals from food due to the demineralisation in farm soil and supermarket processing for longer shelf life.

Nutrition Fact vs. Nutrition Fiction

With all the marketing around food, it can be hard to sort the nutrition fact from the nutrition fiction. Here are a few examples:

"As part of a healthy diet"

The corporations who produce fast food and fizzy drinks, will tell you that they can be enjoyed 'as part of a healthy diet', something I'm sure you've seen on food packaging. It's very hard for your body if you incorporate sugary, fizzy drinks even on a semi-regular basis. Some 'soft' drinks contain as much as 11-14 spoons of sugar in 500ml.

There are plenty of foods disguised as healthy that are actually very unhealthy for you. Fruit juices are a prime example. Some claim to be 'one of your 5-a-day' and in many cases they're full of sugar. It's much better to eat a piece of fruit, then you know you're really getting a portion of fruit!

The dairy industry has also been telling us, for a long time, that milk and cheese are good for us and are an essential part of a healthy diet. However, dairy is heavily processed. By the time it gets to the shops, it's been processed and pasteurised therefore much of the nutritional content is reduced or less easily assimilated by the body. Contrary to popular belief, you don't get enough calcium or other vitamins from it. However grass-fed, raw milk and butter from a farm, are packed full of Omega-3s, Vitamin K-2 and Vitamin D. So, it all comes down to the source. On the flip side there are potentially risks of bacteria in raw milk. Some people choose to avoid dairy altogether and get alternative products instead.

"Fats are bad for you"

You've probably also heard that fats are bad for you. However, there are good fats and bad fats and we often get confused about what fats are what. So, what we want are the healthy fats (according to the alkaline diet) it's the good fats that make us alkaline. The fats that we find in certain meats, processed foods, certain oils, are bad for us. Unfortunately, what many people do nowadays is go fat-free. The problem with going fat-free is that you are actually cutting so much fat out of your diet that you can actually become deficient in your essential fats. Our healthy fats are essential to everything that we do, they are a key food group. Oily fish, avocados, nuts, seeds, olive oil and coconut oil all contain good fats, mainly Omega 3. Omega 3 is anti-inflammatory, alkalising and a fundamental building block for all cell function. We need a much higher source of Omega 3 than of Omega 6 and 9. Too much Omega 6 and 9 (found in processed foods) are pro-inflammatory.

Products that claim to be 'zero percent fat' or 'fat free', are often pumped with chemicals or sugar to replace the fat. These chemicals can be more damaging to the body than the fats! Sweeteners may be sugar free, yet they can increase your hunger and appetite. Healthy nutritious food actually triggers a message to your body to suppress the appetite at the right time once the nutrients have been assimilated.

Fat also helps with the absorption of nutrients. A study showed that eating vegetables with butter helped the absorption of the vitamins and minerals. This is because some vitamins, such as Vitamin D, are fat-soluble, so if we're not having fat, we don't absorb them. Healthy fats are also our main fuel for our brain, so we can't have healthy brain function without them. Studies have found a connection between Omega 3 deficiency and dementia.[19]

---

19 Greg M. Cole, Qui-Lan Ma and Sally A. Frautschy, 'Omega-3 fatty acids and dementia', *Prostaglandins, Leukotrienes Essential Fatty Acids*, 81, no.2-3 (2009), pp.213-221

"You need lower cholesterol"

There's a fair bit of confusion about good cholesterol and bad cholesterol. Good cholesterol builds cells, whereas bad cholesterol damages them. High levels of bad fats can mean that you're not getting enough good fats such as Omega 3. You can lower your levels of bad cholesterol by eating more good fats.

Always be wary of products labelled 'lower cholesterol', 'low fat' and 'free from...' as they can still be full of additives and chemicals; don't let packaging and advertising tell you how to eat! Listen to your body.

"You need calcium to protect against osteoporosis"

Osteoporosis causes brittle bones and it affects more women than men due to the role of different hormones. You do need calcium to help build and maintain strong bones, however, calcium needs Vitamin C and Vitamin D3 to be absorbed, as well as K2 and protein, so if you just take calcium on its own, it won't help your bone health. Now remember, vitamins D and K need fat (Omega 3) to be absorbed!

The latest research into vitamin D suggests that most people in the UK are vitamin D deficient particularly during the winter months and Public Health England has suggested we need a minimum of 400IU per day, interestingly however, the latest research shows that the average adult needs approximately 2000-5000IU

per day depending on their current vitamin D levels and weight. Due to living in the UK, this is one area I would expect people to need supplementation in.

Dairy is not necessarily the only source of calcium. Dark, leafy greens, salmon, beans, lentils, nuts and seeds also have good amounts of calcium. If you haven't got enough Vitamin C, D3 and K2 then it results in not enough calcium being absorbed into the bone, leading to increased calcium deposits in the arteries. This can lead to calcified arteries which can cause cardiovascular disease. It really is important to get the balance of your nutrition right.

Leading Vitamin D researchers have advised that in most cases it is much more important to supplement Vitamin D than calcium as you can generally get enough calcium from your food.

"All sugar is bad"

Much like fats, there are good and bad sugars and understanding the difference can transform your health. Your brain needs glycosylation to function. It helps you to concentrate and make decisions. There is some confusion over sugar from fruit and whether it's good or not. Some people think that juicing is bad because you get all of the sugar. There are different kinds of sugars (fructose, glucose, lactose and sucrose, to name a few) While you get nutrition and vitamins from fruit you get the most benefits from vegetable sugars.

Sugar that you need to avoid is white processed sugar. So, don't add sugar to your food or drinks. Alcohol is also processed as a sugar and it depletes your B vitamins due to the effects it has on the lining of the digestive tract and the liver. The damaging effects of too much processed sugar has been reported to create insulin resistance and lead to both Type 2 diabetes, which can ultimately lead to heart disease and the increased risk of stroke and Type 3 diabetes which is the new proposed name for Alzheimer's Disease due to the effects of insulin resistance on brain neurons.

There are plenty of wonderfully naturally sweet vegetables out there. Carrots, sweet potato, beetroot... these vegetables can give you the sweet boost you need. Naturally occurring sugars are healthier for you and important, because with fruits and vegetables you also get soluble fibre, which affects the way sugar is absorbed. You should be mindful of the balance between fruits and vegetables in your diet though. If you're blending or juicing, try to keep a ratio of 80% veg and 20% fruit. Again, you can tweak the ratio slowly to let your palette adjust. Start by making a basic carrot and apple juice with equal amounts of both, then gradually change to using more carrot. Over time, you can start adding less sweet flavours, such as spinach and kale.

"Don't eat salt"

Many people believe that salt is bad for you. However, it's not just salt that's the problem, it's the sodium. Processed table salt is very high in sodium, it is healthier to avoid this. If you replace it with Himalayan rock salt, you'll be getting a blend of good quality minerals.

Most processed foods have high quantities of added salt or sugar, so it is generally best to avoid adding extra salt to these types of meals and, if possible, avoid processed meals altogether. However, if most of your food is freshly prepared then adding small amounts of Himalayan salt would be a better alternative to table salt.

"Eat your 5-a-day!"

We actually need more like 17-21 a day! An easy way to increase your nutrient content is by juicing. Due to the poorer quality of soil now due to over-cultivation, you need to eat much more to get the same nutritional value from one piece of fruit or vegetable compared to

20-30 years ago. Additionally, if you compare the taste and colour of the cheaper mass-produced vegetables with organic, in most cases you will notice that mass produced vegetables seem to taste watery and have less flavour. Research suggests that there are 20-40% more antioxidants in organic food. The problem with 5-a-day is the product labelling is ambiguous and in some cases on items that are unhealthy for you. It has really become a marketing exercise by food companies and shops rather than the quality of the food itself.

The benefits from eating fresh fruit and vegetables are huge. It has been shown to reduce the risk of heart disease, cancer and diabetes. However, unfortunately the average household in the UK was estimated to only have 3 ½ potions per day. This is another reason why I love and recommend juicing. It's a quick and easy way to get your daily quota of vegetables!

"Carbs are bad for you"

There are so many low carbohydrate diets out there and lots of confusion over whether or not you need carbs. Well, you do! They give you energy and good quality carbs can aid digestion. However, we don't need many starchy carbs and we need to balance the amount of carbs we eat with good quality sources of protein and fats. You get carbs from vegetables, so you don't really need to eat lots of fillers such as bread and pasta. You'll end up in a 'carb-coma', where your blood sugar crashes because you've eaten too many carbs and not enough fat and protein. In fact, you don't really need to think too much about getting enough carbohydrates, as we naturally eat many sources, it's just as important not to actively try and cut them out completely or your body can go into a state called ketoacidosis, this leads to increased acidity in the blood and it can damage your kidneys and other organ systems. A good diet is all about a healthy balance between the food groups.

"Recommended Daily Allowance (RDA)"

I'm sure you've seen this on food packaging and the back of vitamin boxes. RDA refers to the recommended daily allowance of certain vitamins and minerals. However, this measure takes nutrition out of context and results in confusion. The health authorities came up with this at the start of the Second World War, when they were doing rationing and they decided on the minimum levels of vitamins and minerals necessary to have before you became diseased. The recommendations are actually at the lowest level. This is a bit like the 5-a-day myth, you often need much more than the RDA indicates for a number of nutrients, especially if you are deficient. Make sure to check with a professional who understands nutrition as to what's right for you.

A question that can change the way you think is:

'Compared to what?'

In other words asking, "is this healthy compared to what?" will help you mindfully look at the food you are eating and make a healthier choice.

SUMMARY: Performance

Once you've started to think about your food as your Fuel to THRIVE®, you'll start to change your eating habits. So many symptoms of health problems are rooted in the diet. If you think about it, your diet is one of the easiest things you can change, it's just a matter of changing what you do when you go to the supermarket.

There are simple steps you can take to change your nutritional mindset.

It's important to enjoy life and enjoy your body. Don't beat yourself up if you do make the occasional unhealthy choice as the stress hormones you will release are also detrimental. Just notice what you are eating and at least 90% of the time you want to eat healthily to get the most out of life and really THRIVE.

There are lots of nutritional fictions out there, so try not to be swayed. Stick to whole foods most of the time, rather than packaged, processed food. Just look at a food and ask yourself this simple question: Is this going to cleanse me or clog me? What could I eat as an alternative?

How can your car run properly if it doesn't have the right fuel and if you were driving without taking time to stop for fuel, how far do you think you could go before you broke down? Our bodies need the right fuel to function at their best.

Why not look up a new healthy recipe today, or buy a vegetable or herb you'd never normally cook with and use it this evening? Have fun playing with new healthy foods and you'll begin to notice the difference to both your performance and health.

PART 5:

STEP UP & T.H.R.I.V.E.™

Find your Passion

Thriving is about being able to do the best you possibly can given your circumstances. It's about living an optimum wellness lifestyle, which gives you the ability to Step Up & THRIVE™. What does it take to Step Up & THRIVE™? Consistency: making your health a priority and changing it from a 'maybe' to a 'must'.

We've already discussed why your health is important to you and how it affects your life. So how can you make this into a reality? What does it take to make it actionable? Well, it needs you to step up. You need to set a new standard of what you want to achieve. Then, you need consistent and continuous action to achieve it.

The first thing you need to do is commit some time every week, every day, or every couple of days towards different elements. It could be working on your physical health through exercise, or your mindset through journaling. There are many different things you could do and I wouldn't recommend doing them all at once. It's my belief, that it's best to start with getting a chiropractic check-up and adjustments. Then, you can start to build in exercise and the right nutrition and think about areas of your lifestyle that might be causing you stress.

Once you understand your habits and their implications for your health, you can work on breaking old habits and building new ones. You then need to focus on repeating those habits over a course of time and rescheduling your life to set yourself up for success in whatever area you want to excel and THRIVE in. In other words, you need to ignite your knowledge. Putting your understanding of your health and your body into practice requires passion, a spark to really get that driving force going.

When you feel that spark, you get excited and keep moving forward. It could be that you're creating new nutrition recipes for you and your family. It might be that you've started doing a new type of exercise that's making you feel great, or that you've set yourself a new goal or challenge, such as doing a walk for charity or running 5k in a specific time. You've got to figure out what excites you so that you want to keep going.

It's important to keep moving forward because of your values. You need to think about and reaffirm your values in case there are any limiting beliefs still lurking around. Ask yourself how you thought about your health before and what's changed? Why did you decide to make a change? What values do you now hold about your health? What's more important to you now - going out and getting fast food and a pint, or taking great care of your health? Watching countless episodes of something on T.V, or doing some exercise to energise you? Don't focus on what others think, it's more a question of what is important in your own life. It all comes down to the Pareto's Principal, 80/20: 20% of what you do is going to get 80% of the result. It's really important to regularly re-assess your current circumstances to make sure that you are moving towards your highest values as much as possible. Your habits and circumstances that served you well 20 years ago might not necessarily be right for you at this point in time.

Consider this: people used to believe that it wasn't possible to run a four-minute mile. Then in 1954, Roger Bannister ran a mile in 3:59.4. The 'four-minute barrier' has since been broken by many athletes and is now the standard of all male professional middle distance runners. Sometimes, we find that it's exactly the same for your health. You don't necessarily know what standard of health is possible until you learn more about your body and challenge your beliefs.

If you haven't known anybody have improvement with a condition like the one you're suffering with, or if you haven't known anybody who lacks energy like you do turn things around, you might not know that there's hope: that your health and energy levels can be improved and optimised. From working with thousands of patients, I have helped people consistently get great results. You too can set a new standard for your health today.

The final aspect of THRIVE is education. I strongly encourage you to go out and educate yourself. You've just learnt a great deal about health. Please don't let this book be the only source of information. Come to one of our courses or go on another course that suits you to learn even more about your health. Invest in your education about your health and make it your own personal study.

Let's look at what it means to T.H.R.I.V.E™ in more detail, by considering the following principles: **T**ime, **H**abits, **R**epetition, **I**gnite, **V**alue, **E**ducation.

Time

You might be thinking; how will I have time for all of this? I'm already busy and stressed. We all have the same amount of time: 24 hours in a day. Time is a resource that can go by very quickly and easily. Many people talk about how life flies by. It seems to go so fast, especially in this 'nano-second culture' that we've created. There are so many demands and pressures on us, whether it's in work or in relationships, it can feel like our time isn't our own anymore. So, what you need to do is commit to spending quality time with you. That's right, **YOU**.

Having that time, even if it's fifteen minutes, half an hour, or an hour a day, where you're really focusing on your health or your mindset is invaluable. It's not about focusing on the problem; it's about focusing on the solution. It's about investing the time that you have wisely by making it effective for you. When I discuss with my patients about the importance of committing time and energy to focus on their health, some find it hard. Unless they are in crisis mode, they believe that they simply haven't got enough time. However, you can 'save' so much time by changing the way you do things. For example, if you're going for a long car journey or exercising, you could simultaneously listen to an audio book or a health or mindset podcast at the same time, so your car becomes your university on wheels. It's also important to make the most of time by engaging with your loved ones and being present in the moment. How many times has your mind wandered off thinking about work or what you need to do instead of connecting and being present with the person you are with?

Learning techniques to manage your time effectively is one thing, however, you also really need to schedule it. Put it in the calendar and stick to your commitment to spend time focusing on your health. It's not just about *making* time, it's about choosing how you use your time, being intentional. Most people are great at keeping an appointment with someone else, yet they can find it difficult to keep that commitment for scheduling time with themselves. Start prioritising time for your health!

Habits

Choosing to spend time on yourself largely comes down to breaking habits. We all have habits, behaviours we repeat on a daily basis and as we know, there are good habits and bad habits. Sometimes, it's not immediately obvious which is which (some bad habits can make us feel good, temporarily at least). Take time to pause and think about which habits are supportive for good health and your overall well-being and which are destructive.

As I mentioned earlier on in the book, if you have the same repetitive posture for a long period of time, it's going to create a habit, which is therefore going to create strain that can lead to neck problems or lower back problems. Whereas, changing your posture and moving around differently will make a huge difference to your alignment and your body overall.

The habits that you create make a huge difference to your body and health. As we learnt in Part 4 of this book, from a nutritional point of view, if you eat the wrong food in the morning, you then feel a drop in energy, which creates a craving for more unhealthy food, which then leads to another drop in blood sugar, which then leads to more fatigue. Your eating habits affect your energy on a day-to-day basis.

Your brain is amazing. It is wired to create success and find ways to make your tasks easier. As a result, we find ways to shortcut things. For example, you go to a restaurant and end up ordering the same food, or you put your trousers on in the morning only to put the same leg in first every time. Changing habits can therefore feel quite uncomfortable. If you cross your arms one way, then try changing them and crossing them the other way it will feel awkward because you've done it the other way thousands of times before.

In the same way, changing a habit when it comes to investing in yourself is likely to be uncomfortable at first. Unless you've had a major life experience that has challenged you and made you determined to change everything, finding the motivation to change habits can be difficult. So, how do you do it when you're comfortable?

First, you need to have clarity on what you want to change. That means developing a conscious awareness of what's actually going on in the first place and identifying which aspects of your behaviour might be leading to the problem. I had one patient, for example, who was having sleepless nights as a result of their neighbours making noise. Their stress response became a habit, so they routinely felt stressed at bedtime. They felt disempowered by the situation, which led to stress and depression. Compelling their neighbours to stop making noise wasn't possible (since the noise level was not above the legal limit) and they didn't want to move house, so they had to resolve the issue by focusing on what they could control: their habits and behaviour. It was only when they started to change their own habits and work on their mindset that their stress response started to change. The actual situation remained the same, however they've improved the quality of their sleep and their health by working on creating a new habit. In their case, the new habit they created was using BrainTap for sleep and stress reduction on a regular basis. As a result, their mindset changed and they identified when they used to feel like a victim they were much more stressed. Now they recognised that they were in control of their thoughts, the stress response had stopped being fired off as often.

When you're working on creating new habits, there are always situations in life that knock you off the path. You can help yourself to stay on track by surrounding yourself with the resources you need, whether it's your exercise programme, your nutritional programme, whether it's reading or listening to something that inspires you, going to a seminar or being around like-minded friends. If you make an effort to keep these resources around you, you'll notice how much better you feel. In terms of your brain, these small changes in behaviour start to lay new neurons down and open up new dopamine pathways, giving you positive rewards, which stimulates memory, motivation, emotion and allows these new habits to be formed.

Say, for example, someone wants to get into the habit of running. They know that they enjoy running and they'd love to start doing it regularly, however it's not become a habit yet. Instead, they habitually sit down and watch TV in the evening. How do they change their habit from watching TV to starting exercise? The first point is recognising that they want to change it. The second point is actually looking at their values by asking themselves what's more important, watching another episode of a mundane TV show or doing something that they know is going to nurture their health, concentration and energy levels.

Once you've initiated a new type of behaviour, it's important to maintain it in order for it to become a habit. To do this, it's helpful to keep returning to your values and resources. I have helped a number of patients who came into the clinic who, having become very motivated to start running, have developed knee or ankle injuries which have prevented them from running. Since they couldn't run, they gave up all exercise, instead of switching and doing another exercise until they recovered. If you're in this situation and you remind yourself that, although you love running, fundamentally it is a behaviour you're adopting as a route to good health, it will help you to stay on track and think about what other types of exercise you can do whilst you are recovering. Having assessed a patient, I can recommend other types of movement to keep them healthy and aid their recovery. If you had the resources to run, whether that's in the gym, on the treadmill or outside in the park, you've got the resources for other exercise, whether that's by using different equipment in the gym, doing particular stretches or walking, or even taking up swimming instead of running.

Maslow's concept of 'unconscious incompetence' also comes into play here. In other words, you don't know what you don't know. Once you realise that things aren't quite right, you then move to conscious incompetence, where you know that you don't know something (even if you still don't know what that something is!). Then, once you get shown how to do something, you reach a stage of conscious competence. Take driving a car as an example. At first, you don't know what you need to know in order to drive. Then, after a few lessons you are aware of what you don't know, because you've learnt a bit about how a car works and what you have to do, then, after a whole course of lessons and studying, you know how to drive - you understand the different components of knowledge required and it comes together as a whole giving you the ability to do it. You get to a point where you don't really have to think about the individual actions you're taking to drive the car, you just do it! This behaviour, where you're doing something competently without consciously thinking about it, is known as muscle memory. When you reach this stage, a shift has taken place in your brain. It's the same with learning any musical instrument, a sport, or a set of postural exercises.

The cortex, the thinking part of the brain, actually changes and rewires messages to the cerebellum. The cerebellum is the part that's involved in learned responses. When this happens, you've reached unconscious competence and you'll do things as muscle memory, rather than thinking about doing it.

I'd add something to this concept of unconscious competence though. I like to encourage mindful competence. Mindful competence is when you actively try to maintain an awareness of what you're doing, even when you're doing it out of muscle memory and are not having to think about it. So, for example, let's say you've now learned to drive. You can drive somewhere on autopilot, without having to think about it. The problem with that is that if you live your life on autopilot, you can miss some of the great things. You'll get more value out of everyday life if you are mindful and really work on being present in the moment. For example, earlier I suggested that you could listen to an audio book while you're exercising to save time. However, at the same time, you also might want to be really present with your body while you're doing the exercise, so you can feel the messages your body is giving you and learn what stretches it and what feels good. Different actions work for different people, it's about working out what works for you - what makes a habit enjoyable and easy enough for you to continue with it once you've reached a stage of unconscious competence.

Habits can be empowering or disempowering; resourceful or unhelpful. Your response to stress can trigger different habits. For example, the feeling of stress might trigger you to want to smoke, drink alcohol or go into a rage. You can challenge your habits by asking, are they supportive? Are they destructive? Are they empowering or disempowering? Then, you can consciously decide that when something happens in the future to make you feel stressed, your new default response will be something different. Imagine if, instead of triggering you to do something destructive, your stress response triggered you to go for a run or talk to a friend.

So, if you want to change a habit, you need to create enough leverage to make that change important enough for you to succeed. Do you remember the 'Uncle Joe' story I mentioned earlier in the book, about a person who seemed fit and healthy, but died suddenly without warning? When I told that story at a seminar, one of my patients came up to me afterwards and told me his story. He said that he had had a heart attack at 52 years old. It wasn't the conversation with their doctor about quitting smoking, or even the fact that they had the heart attack that stopped them from smoking. The catalyst that helped him change and transform his health was when his eleven-year old daughter said, "Daddy, stop smoking otherwise you won't be around to walk me down the aisle when I get married". Sometimes we do more for someone else than we do for ourselves. Once you've found out what's important to you and what you value, you can utilise it to reach a deeper level of importance, giving you the leverage to create change.

Once you've come to understand your habits, identify what you want to change and make a conscious decision to change them in a positive way for your health and well-being. After that, it's time to start building in repetition.

Repetition

'If at first you don't succeed try, try and try again'. You've probably heard this phrase before. It's what Robert the Bruce, King of Scotland, is meant to have told his troops shortly before defeating the English at Bannockburn in 1314. It's said to have been inspired by a spider stoically weaving its web as the King sheltered in a cave. This idea of perseverance still strikes a chord with many people and has been credited with great success. Tony Robbins, for example, said that "repetition is the mother of all skill." The way that I see it as a chiropractor is that, by repeating something over and over again you start to build functional capacity, neurological capacity and conditioning. In other words, you literally re-wire the brain and nervous system giving you greater ability to perform at a higher level.

As we learned earlier on in the book, you can build strength, stability and stamina by starting to exercise and continuing with it over time, which gradually builds muscle. The same thing can happen with your habits. When you make a decision and take small steps towards achieving it you create momentum and drive. As a result, you start to see the results and begin moving towards what you've been aiming to achieve.

That's why it's important to start doing things in a way that you can repeat. Start building your new, productive habits, whether it's journaling each morning, or getting up to do exercise, into a pattern that fits into your day. Having a measurement process can also work really well for some people. There are so many options for tracking your progress with fitness, for example, having a fitness tracker or a smart watch, both of which will generate data on your progress and send you reminders on a regular basis.

When you're doing something regularly and repetitively it's normal to make mistakes. That is why it is important when you're repeating something to give yourself the time to take stock and reflect and don't be hard on yourself if you slip up, just use it as feedback to refocus. Ask yourself, is this working? Is this improving? Do you need to add a new exercise in or take an exercise out? Sometimes, when you're repeating something you can, as we discussed in the section on habits, end up doing things on autopilot. It's important to maintain your awareness and listen to your body. When you're doing particular types of exercise, for example, it's important to check your posture to make sure that it has a positive effect on your body.

When chiropractors work with patients, for example, they look at the adjustment process and refine it as new needs develop. The adjustments that got someone out of pain initially might be different to the adjustments that are needed to maintain their health. It's about building reflection into the repetitive process. Do you remember Archie's story? Repeating exercises over time and doing repetitive adjustments built up his strength and helped move him towards better health. The same is true for Anna's story. Repeated adjustments strengthened her core muscles, helping her through her second pregnancy.

You can actually train your brain in repetition. I'm sure you've smelled a particular perfume or aftershave before or listened to a particular song and it has triggered a memory, taking you right back to where you were when you first experienced it. You can use repetition to change your mood as well. For example, if you listen to certain types of music when doing cardiovascular exercise your brain will associate that music with feeling lively and energised. Then, if you sit down to do something that you normally procrastinate with, yet you listen to that same music, your brain will feel awake and energetic, as if you're about to exercise and you will approach your task differently.

Of course, sometimes people break the cycle of positive repetitive behaviour. When this happens, don't get disheartened. Just re-focus on the things that you value and re-engage with your purpose and why you made that decision to change in the first place.

If you're not sure where to start, visit the resources area and download my 'Morning Power Routine' to help you set up your day positively in a way you can repeat.

Ignite

Once you've worked out your time, reorganised your habits and have started to create and repeat new habits, it's time to ignite the process. That means really fuelling your new lifestyle: finding that burning desire that makes change a must for you. It means really tapping in to your WHY to keep yourself motivated.

A technique that you might find helpful was developed by Nathaniel Branden, a leading psychotherapist and pioneer in the psychology of self-esteem. Branden believes that self-esteem is a human psychological need. If this need is not fulfilled, it can result in problems such as anxiety, depression and difficulty in relationships. He defined self-esteem as 'the disposition to experience oneself as competent to cope with the basic challenges of life and as worthy of happiness'.[20] What's crucial about this definition is the emphasis it places on the individual to work on their own self-esteem. Whilst loved ones - friends, family and partners - are important in helping you to nurture and sustain your self-esteem, it is fundamentally generated by practices carried out by you.

---

20 Nathaniel Branden, *The Six Pillars of Self-Esteem* (n.pl: Bantam 1995), p.27

To help people work on their self-esteem as an active practice, Branden developed these 'Six Pillars of Self-esteem':

- Living consciously: the practice of being aware of what you are doing while you are doing it, i.e., the practice of mindfulness.
- Self-acceptance: the practice of owning your thoughts, emotions and behaviour; of being kind to yourself and respecting yourself.
- Self-responsibility: the practice of owning your actions and fully realising your potential to bring about the change that you want.
- Self-assertiveness: the practice of treating your needs and interests with respect and of expressing them in appropriate ways.
- Living purposefully: the practice of formulating goals and of making and implementing plans to achieve them.
- Personal integrity: the practice of maintaining alignment between your behaviour and beliefs.

Your reasons for changing and maintaining a change are going to be different from other people's. To really develop these points into actions, Branden recommends carrying out sentence completion exercises related to the six pillars. Why not try some now, drawing on what you've learnt in this book so far about your physical, mental and emotional health, your purpose and your habits? Here are some sentences you can try to complete:

Living a healthy and optimum life is important to me because ...

Mindful competence to me means...

The action steps I will take today are...

I get inspired when...

I am grateful when...

If I put time aside for myself today...

I love spending time...

If I immerse myself with healthy resources...

If I surround myself with healthy people...

How did you get on? Have you made it easy to achieve success or have you made it difficult?

These are just suggestions; you can make up your own sentences. Don't think too much about how to complete them, just write them then go back to them a week later and reflect on how that action has changed your habits, behaviour and well-being. It could help you to really think about why your health is important and motivate you to keep repeating the habits that are going to enable you to THRIVE. You could even write these sentences down as a letter and organise for it to be posted to you 6 months later to remind yourself why it's so important to work on your health and what you've made a commitment to do.

What really ignites you? The spark that will keep you going is different for different people. For me, it's about purpose - it's my reason to get up in the morning and do what's important. Finding what ignites you is about tapping into your own reasons to enjoy, to love, to be passionate about what you're doing, whether it's work, hobbies or exercise. Rather than just doing something because you're just doing it, it means actually living life to the full and enjoying that process - even the difficult things. In the past I didn't enjoy exercise, I enjoyed the feeling I had after the exercise, however, what you find is when you've been exercising for a while you start enjoying it as well. It's about pushing your comfort zone and what you find is that as that stretches and changes, you develop new behaviours.

One of my personal examples stems from when I was bullied between the ages of six and eighteen. After that experience, I knew that it was really important for me to make a difference to people. So, I decided to go out into our community and run workshops for different groups of people. The challenge was that I had a fear of speaking, so my first few talks were not comfortable. I felt fear; however, I was determined to get over that fear and I did. Gradually, the more I talked, the better the feedback, the better the results and the better the experience I had. I realised that it was fulfilling something really important, which for me was about helping others.

Once I knew that I was able to contribute to the community by sharing a message and helping people, something shifted. I actually started to really love speaking and, as a result, I was awarded the International Chiropractor of the Year award in 2012 for services to the profession and Professional Speakers Academy Speaker of the Quarter 2018; I even found myself on stage, teaching chiropractors from all over Europe about speaking.

So, I created a new habit, speaking to share a message and help others and gave myself the resources to sustain it. What's your purpose? What ignites you? It could be losing weight, getting an exercise programme in place, reducing your stress levels, getting out of pain. Creating habits to allow you to live in alignment with your purpose will allow you to live a healthy and optimum life, which will enable you to be the best you can for you, your loved ones and your community.

Value

Keeping sight of your purpose is really about knowing what you value and staying true to it. When people think of the word value, they might initially think 'money', yet it means so much more than that. Value is the importance you place on something: your health, time, friends, family. What's important to you? What are your values?

Your values are your organising principles in life. As we said in the earlier section, we all have the same number of hours in a day. You can do many things with your time; however, time is limited. Your values can help you to rank the order of importance of everything in your life, so that you can make the things that really matter to you a priority. If we lose sight of our values, or they become distorted in some way and we're not working towards them, we can get stressed. When our life experiences don't meet with our values, that can create pain and suffering. So, it's not just about identifying what you value, but finding a way to prioritise it, so you can have more time doing what's important for you and for the people you love.

If quality family time is important to you, for example, yet you don't have enough time for it, you'll experience feelings of stress. In that situation, some people settle. They accept the situation, give up on something that's important to them and life becomes boring, mundane and tiring as a result. The alternative is to find a way to move back towards your value of quality family time. Sometimes it takes a crisis to initiate this change, something happening that forces people to pay attention to what really matters.

I'd encourage you to invest some time, the time that I hope you've now decided to put aside for yourself on a regular basis, thinking about what your values are.

However, I'd like to make a suggestion. Since you're reading this book, you probably value your health. I hope so, because with great health, what would you be able to do? Or without good health, what wouldn't you be able to do?

Health is a fundamental value – it's the foundation upon which you can build and develop other values. It's important to think about and define your values because they will create your life experience. If you place a high amount of value on something, by thinking about it and prioritising it, you'll effectively wire your brain to spend time doing those things.

If you're spending time on things that aren't important, you won't feel as fulfilled in life. At the same time, if you spend too much time on one area that's important to you, other areas might suffer as a result, so it's about having a balance in your values as well. So, how do you go about defining and creating your values?

First, you start to build a clear idea of the things you might like to do: your dreams, vision, mission. Then, you divide these into subgroups of different categories. For example, they could be:

Health and wellness

Work, career or mission

Family, friendships and relationships

Recreation, sports, dancing or other physical challenges

Play, which for some could be experiences, others might be the latest gadgets or shopping

Creativity, including art, music or writing

Financial well-being through wealth creation

Giving back, whether through donating time or money

Or spirituality

Of course, these values are related. Wealth can be strongly related to your career and play can be linked to recreation or creativity, all of the above categories have different meanings for different people. You might value all of the above to differing degrees. Certainly, balance in itself is a very important value. Play with these topics and choose 5-6 areas to focus on.

You might remember from earlier in the book that I suffered from fatigue in my early 20s. Energy was high on my values list, yet I hadn't prioritised health. As a result, I sought to get energy from sources such as sugar, caffeine and processed food. However, when I began to reassess my values and I placed health higher up on my list, I began to ask different questions about how to get energy. I asked myself how I could get energy, while at the same time respecting my health. It's important to recognise that sometimes our values can be in conflict. However, as you start to work out what your values are, you begin to discover different strategies for building them into your life.

It is best to have a balance of values. This means organising your life in a way that gives plenty of opportunities to enrich your life experience. It's not easy to achieve a sense of balance though. We're all naturally drawn to some activities over others and sometimes it might feel as though we have to work against our instincts to get a sense of balance. For example, some people, such as business owners and entrepreneurs, will value work and wealth creation highly. They might be very passionate and excited about their business and love developing it. As a result, they spend a great deal of time working on it. If things are out of balance, this can take them away from other very important areas of their life, such as their health or relationships. If they don't work to address this, one of these areas of their life might get to crisis point.

This situation can be avoided by thinking about all of your values and remembering that your health is at the foundation. Really committing to your values might mean making yourself take time away from your business, even though you really want to continue working on it, in order to exercise, or spend time with your family. Or, it could work the other way around.

The real key to sustainable success and fulfilment comes from a healthy balance of your values. If your recreation, such as creative pursuits, are what you really value, you might have to make yourself stop and take stock of your career and long-term financial situation to check that you are also giving them the time and focus you need in order to be secure in the long-run.

Values aren't always clear-cut. We often set up rules of how we obtain fulfilment with a certain value, without even consciously thinking about it. For example, someone might really value the quality of their relationships and family life. Their way of giving value to that might be by providing for the family, so they strive to become successful and create wealth. However, as a result, the one thing they value most, their family, gets pushed away because they're spending more time in the office than with them. This could create stress within the relationship, especially if other family members don't fully understand that creating wealth is actually their way of providing for the family. For example, if their partner has quality time as a high value and work or career isn't particularly high on their list, they might not understand that their partner is trying to share and provide through their work. It's easy to see how different personality types and perceived importance of values can lead to friction or even conflict in a relationship. It is necessary to communicate your values and understand other people's model of the world.

Everybody has a blueprint for their health, work and recreation. In each area of your life you will have rules, beliefs and values that define that area. This subconscious blueprint creates your thoughts, which leads to your feelings and then ultimately your actions and results. For example, some people's blueprint for their exercise is positive because they have decided to value it highly. Their thoughts might include, "exercise energises me, it helps me to concentrate and makes me feel good," or perhaps they play team sports and they value it because of the sense of camaraderie they get. They might feel more connected to other people after participating in sports or group training. Other people might have a negative blueprint for exercise. Perhaps they see it as something that they should do, or maybe they associate it with injury. This lack of priority or limiting belief might subsequently create negative thoughts around exercise, meaning that they're obviously much less likely to do it.

Stress is created when your values conflict. By thinking about and reordering your values, you can set the game up to win. The key is to make it easy for yourself to commit to what you value. If energy or health is a really high priority on your values list, the way you would achieve it is called the vehicle you use to get the desired result. For example, going to the gym is a possible vehicle to get fit. Some people find it boring; others look forward to it. Some people feel overwhelmed by the thought of going. They think, I've got to pack my bag, get to the gym, find a locker, work out what I'm going to do there. Other people think, I'm going to grab my bag and go. They've chunked it up into more manageable pieces. Once you get to that point, where you don't really have to think about doing something, it becomes much easier to continue doing it. You forge a new neural pathway that creates a learned response. There are many ways to get fit. So, you can change the chunking to enjoy the gym, otherwise you might need to find a different vehicle for fitness, such as joining a specific group. Personally, I prefer team sports and training with others and generally find exercising on my own harder. To set the game up to win for myself, I joined a karate club and trained regularly for over 10 years rarely missing a session. I even went on 5-day intensive karate training camps.

Our values are often created habitually and we need to break the habit in order to change them or reorder them.

Educate

Educating yourself is about providing yourself with the resources you need to grow and develop and enjoy doing it. The best way to learn is to learn while you're having fun because you'll retain more. Instead of it feeling like a chore, it will feel like something you want to do and that will make it much easier to carry on doing it.

Even as people get older, if they do something new and they learn, they create new neural pathways. For example, if you go to a shop and it's the same one you've always been to, you know where everything is and don't really have to think about it. Whereas, if you go to a new supermarket, it becomes harder to shop because you have to think and look for everything. It's more mentally tiring because you're exercising and developing your brain.

By doing new and varied activities every day such as going to a new supermarket, driving a different way to work, learning a language, doing Sudoku, especially if you're not good with numbers, or the crossword if you're not good with words can really help your brain. Other suggestions could be taking up painting, pottery or dancing. All these new activities stimulate different parts of the nervous system that are involved in learning. When you're learning, you're actually laying new neurological capacity down. So, actually, you're improving your grey matter. To try to improve your brain, really challenge yourself, don't just stick to what you know and what you're good at.

In order to THRIVE, it's important to learn about your health. Invest in developing an understanding of your health, like you've done by reading this book. It's about learning about what's right for you and taking ownership, rather than handing your health over to your doctor, the fitness industry, or other people. I'd recommend you dig deeper towards finding that knowledge of your body and health, you'll do this naturally once you've prioritised your health. There are many great suggestions in this book, so you can go out and experience some of them. Different approaches work for different people, so it's really important that you learn as much as possible and apply it in your life to work out what makes you feel at your best. It's your life, nobody else's. I'm still learning myself through my personal and professional journey. I've shared my insights, however I'm aware that there will always be more to learn. I find that really exciting and interesting and I continue to incorporate new lessons into my seminars and workshops.

To really kick-start your health education, set yourself some health goals. There's nothing like a challenge to really push you forwards, so learn as much as you can about how to live an optimum life and take action. Think of one new area of health to play with and test it out and experiment. Learn new recipes, try new exercises.

Thinking about how you feel, whether you feel good or not, is one initial way to assess your health. Please remember that you can't always measure your health by how you're feeling, because sometimes there are underlying issues. It's about being aware of what you're doing on a daily basis, living mindfully and trying to find balance in your life. If this is your first step towards looking into health in a detailed way, I'd recommend you go to a seminar about health, whether you go elsewhere or come to one of my nutritional or mindset seminars. Keep making the choice to learn and enjoy it!

Take the next step in your learning cycle. I mentioned earlier 'knowledge is power'. Well, I'd say that practical application of knowledge is power. It's not just about knowing something; it's about taking action to embed the knowledge even further and extend it. We all know that it's important to eat vegetables and fruit and I mentioned earlier about the old '5-a-day' campaign. How many people don't even eat a minimum of 5 portions of fruit or vegetables a day? That's because, although people might know the importance of healthy eating in theory, they haven't prioritised it enough to do it in practice and feel the benefits of it. It's just something they're told to do, something they *know* in a technical sense, however, the transition to ***knowing*** in a deeper sense, (in other words when you know something instinctively) means that you don't have to think about it anymore because it becomes part of your daily life, your new norm.

As I recommended earlier on in this book, you don't need to put yourself under pressure to suddenly be the healthiest person in the world straight away. This is about you and how you feel and function—enabling yourself to feel well and energetic so you can live life to the full. That's a pretty amazing goal - it's worth playing the long game for. So, take one or two key steps, then revisit them. Challenge yourself to change your snacks to healthy whole foods, vegetables, fruit or nuts, for example, for a week. Or challenge yourself to go to a new fitness class, or to park further away from your destination and walk a bit further. Use this book as a learning guide that you can keep coming back to.

Educating yourself also really builds your confidence because it gives you trust in what you're doing. If people try to knock you off course (you know the type), the ones who'll say, "oh go on, have another drink", "what are you going to the gym for, boring!", "salad?! You need proper food", you'll have that inner confidence to shrug it off, knowing that you're doing what's best for you and what you really want to be doing, without doubt or fear holding you back. Just continue to take slow, easy steps — there's no need for it to be difficult, it's not about punishing yourself. Make it as easy for yourself as possible. You could even work with a mentor or coach.

Health is a process. You won't just do one exercise and be fit for life. Different structures in your body have different healing and repair times. Often, our ability to heal and repair can be impaired by the 5 Dimensions of Stress. Learn about what those different stresses are, then ask what do you have control over? We always have choice. What meaning are you attaching to particular events? Remember that you can retrain your thought processes, which will affect your outcomes.

For example, Tony Robbins talks about twins that grew up with their father on death row. They were separated at an early age. One ended up happy, with a successful career and a loving family. The other also ended up on death row. When asked, "why has your life turned out the way it has?" They both had the same answer, "with a father like mine, what would you expect?" So, they both gave a different meaning to the same event and it affected their lives in completely different ways. The way you interpret an event really can change the course of life you take.

We always have choice about the meanings we give an event. It can be empowering, or disempowering. If you've had a particular experience in life and you're used to thinking about its negative consequences, questions can help to redirect your thinking. If you ask yourself, what's good about this situation? What could be good about it? Just one small thing? Build and stack the positive things. This method might at least neutralise a negative experience and at best, it can turn one of your darkest days into one of your best days. Start telling yourself different stories about you and your life and you'll change the meaning you attach to particular events. This will change how you feel, what you believe and what outcomes you'll get.

I've studied this as a chiropractor because I've seen many patients who have been involved in terrible accidents, such as car accidents and have multiple injuries. I have worked with patients who have been told they'll never walk again or work again and yet I have helped them walk again, work again and enjoy life. It all comes down to a decision they make about what happened. They start to tell themselves a different story about the incident and work towards getting well rather than accept that they'll never be well again. They set themselves health goals and focus on them each day. They tap into their inner strength, which allows them to achieve what they set out to do. In certain situations, it's very easy to adopt a victim mentality where you think, 'this has happened to me and as a result of that I'm powerless. There's nothing I can do.' The opposite of that and a very powerful way to think, is 'this has happened, this is the event. What am I going to do as a result of it?' This question makes you think about the event in more proactive terms. It gives you some control over what to do next and this can make a world of difference to your quality of life, whatever your circumstances.

In 2010, I met an inspirational man called John Marrable. John had received a spinal cord injury after a fall while climbing in 1967 at the age of 11, which left him paraplegic. When John left hospital in 1968 he joined a club for the disabled and continued to pursue sport. In school, he participated in a number of activities including swimming, discus and track and field. When he wanted to explore martial arts, he approached various clubs in England, but he was told that because he was in a wheelchair, he 'couldn't' do it. This made John even more determined and when he emigrated to New Zealand in 1974, he joined a karate club and began formal lessons.

Twenty years later, I had the opportunity to meet John. He was a fifth dan black belt in karate, a feat rare for any fighter, but almost unheard of for an athlete using a wheelchair. John undertook a demonstration where two able-bodied people attacked him, he was knocked out of his chair, yet he subdued and stopped his attackers and pulled himself back into his chair.

When I met him, John told me that after he was injured, he had a decision to make and he decided to keep his life moving forward and to make his life mean something. John represented New Zealand in paraplegic sport and brought home numerous medals. He continues to teach karate, play table tennis and is actively involved in a charity that helps individuals with disabilities to improve their lives through the physical and mental training in martial arts (Budo).[21]

There are so many inspiring examples of people who have changed their lives through courage and faith. Just look at all of the Paralympic athletes who achieve incredible results through determination and effort. We can all continue to seek positive and empowering alternatives by telling ourselves different stories about our lives.

THRIVE

Think about what you've learned so far in this book. Do you know how to Step Up & THRIVE™?

You have to break through your old habits and patterns of thinking and make your health a higher priority on your values list. Igniting that spark is about finding your passion to really make change happen. Start by understanding your habits and then work out what you want to change and how you'll do it. Don't get put off if change doesn't happen immediately. Tomorrow is a new day. Just stick with it in order to slowly change your habits. Educate yourself so you know what you need to do and then repeat the process.

There are so many things you can build into your life that help you to live with more purpose and more passion. Yet, it's also easy to self-

21 See John's website for more information
John Marrable, *Paraplegic Sport*, n.d. <http://johnmarrable.com/paraplegic-sport>

sabotage. For example, if you continue to tell yourself the old self-limiting stories such as, you're overworked or under-appreciated, that you have bad genes and you haven't had it as easy as other people, you'll continue to see the same results. You need to make a conscious choice that life feels better, then you'll start taking actions to justify that feeling. Success comes from within you, not to you, by changing your story to a positive frame of reference your thoughts or beliefs change, which in-turn changes your feelings, this then changes your actions and behaviours and ultimately the results you create change.

It's all about finding balance. It's a bit like a seesaw. At one end you've got aggravating factors: physical, emotional, environmental, chemical and nutritional stresses. On the opposite side, you've got relieving factors: good food, exercise, sleep, mindfulness, meditation, music etc. What can you do to balance the seesaw and optimise your health? The bigger the stresses, the more proactive you have to be about nurturing your health.

Whatever the condition you have, whether it's back pain, or a genetic condition, there's a range of sufferers. Some people will unfortunately suffer more than others. Why is this? If we look at health in terms of the body's power, posture, purpose, performance and passion, as we have done in this book, we start to appreciate the body's amazing adaptive potential. By changing how you think and what you do, understanding and *changing* your habits, you can optimise your health.

To make the transition from just surviving to THRIVING for life, you need to have a greater physiological and psychological resilience to the 5 Dimensions of Stress. Your body has an incredible capacity to adapt to these stresses however, the healthier we are and the more we reduce these stresses, the more potential our body has to adapt to them. This will give us the best chance to live a healthy and vibrant life.

SUMMARY: Passion

In this chapter, we talked about passion: how to Step Up & THRIVE™

Time is a resource for good health. We all feel short on time - that's not going to change, but even spending fifteen minutes to an hour a day really focusing on your health or your mindset is invaluable. It's about investing the time that you have wisely by making it effective for you and your health.

Habits govern your daily behaviour. Cultivate mindful competence. Keep an awareness of what you're doing, even when you're doing it out of muscle memory and are not having to think about it.

Repetition is the key to changing your habits in the long-run. By repeating something over and over again, you start to build functional capacity. Building new habits takes time, so don't get disheartened if it doesn't happen straight away. Get advice, a clear plan, then commit and repeat to condition your new habit.

Ignite is about finding the burning desire that makes change a must for you. It means really tapping into your 'WHY' to keep yourself motivated. What makes you excited? What and who do you love? Use that spark to motivate yourself every day.

Value is very personal – it's about the things in life that are most important to you. Valuing something means that you prioritise it, so invest some time in identifying your values and work out what you can do through your daily habits to live more in line with them.

Educate means learning and enjoying it! It's not just about knowing something from reading it in a book, it's about seeking knowledge that will help you to feel healthy and, most importantly, putting it into practice.

With that in mind, consider each one of these points and write down three simple things you can do today to help you to Step Up & THRIVE™!

Practical Steps and Conclusion

Your unlimited power lies in your ability to create your thoughts! Your life and circumstances are an exact mirror of the thoughts you allow to dominate your mind. Feed your mind, inspire yourself and work from the inside out. Let's make our lives a masterpiece by building with one thought at a time. Expect miracles.

There are numerous places that you can go to in order to find out more about how to THRIVE with optimal health. Look into different options where you can continue to learn at your own pace using books, videos, blogs, seminars and webinars. If you visit the online resources section at www.5tothrive.co.uk, you'll find links to resources we recommend, as well as details of our own events. It will be updated periodically as you continue your journey to better health.

In the online resources, you'll find the '5 to Thrive Health® Tool'. This helps you to identify your energy levels, your ability to handle stress and your lifestyle choices. It is shown as a 'wheel of life'; the circle represents your life, the whole of you. The different areas on the wheel are the various parts of your life; you could think of them as your values. The idea is to assess your values to see if there are important things that you've been neglecting, or things you've been giving too much of yourself to.

It's important to point out that everything in this book is intended for educational purposes. It is not intended as a way to give yourself a diagnosis in place of seeing a professional.

We've covered a great deal of ground here. I really hope you feel inspired to take the small steps that will make big changes and you are excited about what the future holds for you when you're thriving and living a life of optimal health.

Your body is incredible - it is self-healing and self-regulating. As you'll now know, the first step to thriving is to Power Up! Your Central

Nervous System is fundamental to this. Your nervous system is your master system. It controls every cell, every tissue and every organ in your body and will steer your health goals. Getting your system in S.Y.N.C.™ and rebooting your nervous system restores the body's potential, allowing it to essentially power up. We covered how to do this in Part 1. It's about understanding your symptoms and neurology and getting the right chiropractic care.

Once you've understood your symptoms and had an initial chiropractic assessment, it's time to start thinking about how to maintain your health in the long-term. Posture is the second step to thriving. In the wrong position, your body can become injured and can continue to re-injure itself. Strengthening your body physically can help you to avoid and overcome accidents that you may experience or reduce repetitive strains.

Finding your purpose, your WHY, is the spark that will motivate you each and every day. This is the third step to thriving. Having a strong sense of purpose can help reduce the effects of physical, mental, emotional, environmental and chemical stress, which can affect your heart, blood pressure and memory. Neutralising the stresses that occur in your day-to-day environment can make a big difference to your quality of life.

When you have a strong sense of purpose, you want to get out of bed every day and perform to the best of your ability. Whether that means excelling at work, beating your personal best in running, achieving a certain fitness goal, mastering a new skill or spending more quality time with your family. Whatever it is that drives you, you want to be able to do it to the best of your ability. Of course, you also want to enjoy it! Thriving is about living life to the full and having fun while you're doing it.

Of course, your mental health is just as important as your physical health. You can't separate your body and mind, they are both part of the same system. You can improve your mental health using the Mind Mastery Matrix® and working on the 8 Ms: Mindfulness, Meditation, Music, Memory, Motivation, Mantras, Momentum, Musts.

Our performance on a daily basis is fuelled by what we put into our bodies. In Part 4, we exposed some common myths and misconceptions about food. Eating healthily doesn't have to be difficult or boring. Simple, fresh, unprocessed food will provide your body with all the nutrients it needs to THRIVE and that means lots of colourful, juicy, replenishing vegetables and fruits, along with delicious high-quality fish or meats, whole grains and nuts. Just do most of your shopping in the fresh food aisles of the supermarket and challenge yourself to try out new, healthy recipes. You'll improve your health and learn something new at the same time!

We concluded with Passion and how to Step Up & THRIVE™ by looking after your time, changing habits, creating repetition, igniting the spark, choosing the areas that you value most and continuously learning new and exciting things that will help enrich your life and give you a deeper sense of passion.

After reading this book, do you have the motivation to be healthier? I hope so! Being healthier is achievable for each and every one of us. You're much more likely to achieve your lifestyle goals if you have an incentive or target that you want to reach. Emotional stress, such as fear, anger and depression can hinder your ability to achieve your health goals. Being passionate about your health can help you to clarify your aspirations and give you a more concrete vision of what you need to do to achieve them. It will also make you more motivated to reach them and more driven to make things happen.

Living a life of optimal health is a journey. Just keep moving forwards. Take the advice in this book and build on it as you continue to educate yourself through further reading, seminars or having a mentor or coach. Remember, it's about working out what works for you, how you can be the healthiest, happiest version of yourself.

After all,

> "Why Just Survive When You Were Born To THRIVE?
>
> - Dr Jason Gould

A Letter From Jason

Dear Reader,

I hope you have found this book helpful and have enjoyed our journey together through THRIVE.

Remember, every journey starts with a first step and the good news is, you have already taken that step by investing time in yourself to read this book.

You are empowered with knowledge and options, so don't stop here. Your health and whatever challenges you currently face, CAN be improved and you can keep moving forward towards optimal health for you.

My help and advice does not need to end with this book and I do not intend to leave you to take the next steps of your journey alone.

I invite you to visit me at my family wellness centre, Chislehurst Chiropractic Clinic. If you are new to chiropractic it is a great opportunity to find out more and to see how it can help you. If you are a current patient, we can speak further about your health goals. I'm also happy to talk about the 5 to Thrive Health® system or to answer any questions you may have about this book. Please call us on 0208 295 1733 today and one of my team will book you in. If you aren't able to get to our clinic in Chislehurst, make sure to seek out an excellent chiropractor near you.

There is a wealth of information in the online resources section of the THRIVE book portal, please visit:

www.5tothrive.co.uk

SCAN ME

I also offer a number of courses online, including Fuel to Thrive® and Mind Mastery Matrix®, so wherever you are in the country, you can learn more.

In house at Chislehurst Chiropractic Clinic, I run Mind Mastery Matrix®, a workshop that expands on the topics we covered in Part 3. There are also a number of complimentary workshops with limited spaces on offer at the clinic covering a range of topics including stress, arthritis and optimal sports performance.

If your business, school, sports club or society could benefit from knowing more about some of the topics covered in this book, or if they need further advice in regard to health and wellness, I would be happy to visit you with a bespoke talk for your needs.

Please email jason@5tothrivehealth.com and my team will be happy to arrange any of these things for you.

I wish you all the best on your onwards journey towards optimal health.

Yours in health and wellness,

Jason

Glossary[22]

Acidosis

A condition characterised by an abnormal increase in the acidity of the blood and extracellular fluids.

Alkalising

To make alkaline.

Anterior Head Carriage

When the neck tilts forward and out of alignment with the spine.

Antioxidant

A substance, such as vitamin C, vitamin E, or beta carotene that counteracts the damaging effects of oxidation in a living organism.

Arthritis

Inflammation of a joint or joints characterised by pain and stiffness of the affected parts.

Autoimmune

(Of a disease) caused by the action of antibodies produced against substances normally present in the body.

Biomechanical

Relating to biomechanics, the study of the mechanics of movement in people and animals.

22 Glossary created in part and with thanks using:
Collins English Dictionary online, 2019, <https://www.collinsdictionary.com>

Blood Cholesterol Levels

A measurement of the amount of cholesterol in someone's blood.

Blood Lipid Levels

Level of fatty substances found in the blood.

Bone Spur (Osteophyte)

A small abnormal bony outgrowth.

Bisphenol A (BPA)

A synthetic organic compound used to make plastics and resins.

Bronchitis

Inflammation of the bronchial tubes, characterised by coughing, difficulty breathing, etc, cause by infection or irritation of the respiratory tract.

Carcinogenic

A substance that is carcinogenic is likely to cause cancer.

Catecholamines

Any of a group of hormones that are catechol derivatives, especially adrenaline and noradrenaline.

Cerebellum

One of the major divisions of the vertebrate brain, situated in humans above the medulla oblongata and beneath the cerebrum, whose function is coordination of voluntary movements and maintenance of bodily equilibrium.

Chiropractic Adjustments

A procedure in which chiropractors use their hands or a small instrument to apply a controlled force to a spinal joint. The goal of this procedure is to improve spinal motion and improve your body's physical function.

Chronic Inflammatory Condition

When the body's inflammatory process as a response to perceived injury or infection continues long term or occurs where it is not required.

Coeliac Disease

A chronic intestinal disorder caused by sensitivity to the protein gliadin contained in the gluten of cereals.

Cognitive

Means relating to the mental process involved in knowing, learning and understanding things.

Core

Is relating to groups of muscles that stabilise joints. Back and abdominal muscles stabilise the spine and other core muscles stabilise other joints.

Cortex

The outer layer of any organ or part, such as the grey matter in the brain that covers the cerebrum (cerebral cortex).

Cortisol

Another name for hydrocortisone, the principal glucocorticoid secreted by the adrenal cortex; 17-hydroxycorticosterone.

Dead Lifts

A type of exercise in which a person lifts a barbell off the floor, stands up straight and holds the weight hanging downward at arm's length.

Detoxification

Treatment that is intended to remove toxic substances from the body.

Dexterity

1. Physical, especially manual, skill or nimbleness.
2. Mental skill or adroitness; cleverness.

DNA

Deoxyribonucleic acid; a nucleic acid that is the main constituent of the chromosomes of all organisms (except some viruses).

Dopamine

A chemical found in the brain that acts as a neurotransmitter and is an intermediate compound in the synthesis of noradrenaline.

Electroencephalography (EEG)

An instrument for recording the electrical activity of the brain, usually by means of electrodes placed on the scalp, used to diagnose tumours of the brain, to study brain waves, etc.

Electrogoniometer

An electrical device for measuring angles of joints and their range of motion.

Electromagnetic Fields

A field of force associated with a moving electric charge equivalent to an electric field and a magnetic field at right angles to each other and to the direction of propagation.

Epigenetics

The study of heritable changes that occur without a change in the DNA sequence.

Free Radicals

An atom or group of atoms containing at least one unpaired electron and existing for a brief period of time before reacting to produce a stable molecule.

Gluten Intolerance

Gluten is a protein found in wheat, barley and rye (primarily) and gluten intolerance is characterised by digestive issues after eating gluten, including abdominal pain, bloating, gas and diarrhoea.

Glycol ethers

A large group of organic solvents.

Glycosylation

The process by which sugars are chemically attached to proteins to form glycoproteins.

Grey Matter

The greyish tissue of the brain and spinal cord, containing nerve cell bodies, dendrites and bare (unmyelinated) axons.

HDL

High-density lipoprotein, a lipoprotein that helps remove cholesterol from the bloodstream and that is believed to reduce the risk of heart disease.

High Intensity Interval Training (HIIT)

A cardiovascular exercise strategy alternating short periods of intense anaerobic exercise with less intense recovery periods.

Hippocampus

An area of cerebral cortex that forms a ridge in the floor of the lateral ventricle of the brain, which in cross section has the shape of a sea horse. It functions as part of the limbic system.

Homeostasis

The maintenance of metabolic equilibrium within an animal by a tendency to compensate for disrupting changes.

Hypertonicity

(Especially of muscles) being in a state of abnormally high tension.

Hypotonicity

(Of muscles) lacking normal tone or tension.

Innate Intelligence

It is a pivotal chiropractic concept. Innate intelligence is the automatic inner intelligence and know-how of the body wired into you that governs every single act in your body. Every single chemical reaction, every tissue formation and every healing process.

Insulin

A protein hormone, secreted in the pancreas, that controls the concentration of glucose in the blood.

Joint-play

There are three movements within a joint: active, passive and joint play. Joint play is the accessory movement available within a joint, which is not under voluntary control but is needed for proper functioning of the joint.

Juicing

The action of extracting juice from fruit or vegetables.

Ketoacidosis

A condition in which excessive levels of ketone bodies and glucose cause the blood to become acidic.

Kinematic Chain

A kinematic chain is a group of links either joined together or arranged in a manner that permits them to move relative to one another. If the links are connected in such a way that no motion is possible, it results in a locked chain or structure.

LDL

Low-density lipoprotein. A lipoprotein that carries cholesterol in the blood to the cell tissues and that in excess is believed to increase the risk of coronary artery disease.

Lymphasise

Lymphasising is the use of movement and gravity to stimulate cell cleansing.

Lymphatic System

An extensive network of capillary vessels that transports the interstitial fluid of the body as lymph to the venous blood circulation.

Mechanoreceptors

A type of sensory receptor sensitive to touch, tension, pressure, etc.

Melanoma

A malignant tumour composed of melanocytes, occurring especially in the skin, often as a result of excessive exposure to sunlight.

Melatonin

The hormone-like secretion of the pineal gland, *Melatonin* is a hormone that regulates the sleep–wake cycle.

Metabolic Acidosis

Occurs when the body produces too much acid. It can also occur when the kidneys are not removing enough acid from the body.

Metastasise

(Especially of cancer cells) to spread to a new site in the body via blood or lymph vessels.

Motor Neurone Disease

A progressively degenerative disease of the motor system causing muscle weakness and wasting.

MRI

Short for Magnetic Resonance Imaging.

Neural Plasticity

The ability of the brain to form and reorganise synaptic connections, especially in response to learning or experience or following injury.

Neuro-Acoustic Harmonics

The therapeutic application of sound.

Neurons

A neuron is a cell which is part of the nervous system. Neurons send messages to and from the brain.

Neuropathic Pain

Pain caused by damage or disease affecting the somatosensory nervous system, where pain is generated by the nerve itself.

Neuropeptides

A peptide produced by neural tissue, especially one with hormonal activity.

Neurotoxins

Any of several natural substances that interfere with the electrical activities of nerves, thus preventing them from functioning.

Neurotransmitters

A chemical by which a nerve cell communicates with another nerve cell or with a muscle.

Perfluorinated Compounds (PFCs)

A group of chemicals containing fluorine. They are used to make materials stain and stick resistant and do not break down readily.

Pharmacology

The science of drugs, including their characteristics and uses.

Postural Fatigue Syndrome

Abnormal muscle tone around the joints which over time leads to damage and pain.

Pulmonary Oedema

A build-up of fluid in the lungs.

Sacroiliac (Si) Joints

Of or relating to the sacrum and ilium, their articulation, or their associated ligaments.

Sciatic Nerve

The longest nerve in the body, extending from the back of the thigh down to the calf of the leg.

Scoliosis

An abnormal lateral curvature of the spine, of congenital origin or caused by trauma or disease of the vertebrae or hip bones.

Upper-Crossed Syndrome

Occurs when the muscles in the neck, shoulders and chest become deformed, usually as a result of poor posture.

Vasoconstriction

The narrowing of the walls of blood vessels.

About the Author

Dr Jason Gould

BSc (Hons), MChiro, DC (Doctor of Chiropractic)

Co-Founder of Chislehurst Chiropractic Clinic, Developer of the 5 to Thrive Health® System, International Speaker and Health and Wellness Mentor

Dr Jason Gould co-founded Chislehurst Chiropractic Clinic in 2007 with his business partner and wife, Dr Tara Gibson. The clinic has grown to be a multi-award-winning business, including winning the award for 'Best Business with under 50 employees' in the Bromley Business Awards 2019 and awards for Customer Service in 2018 and 2017.

With a special interest in sports injuries and performance, Jason takes care of elite, professional and amateur sportspeople alike. Amongst a variety of engagements with sports professionals, Jason (a second dan black belt in karate himself) took pride in looking after the England karate squad. He is also passionate about treating local people in his community every day, aged from four days to ninety-nine years young.

Jason also teaches professional and student chiropractors and was awarded Speaker of the Quarter at the Professional Speakers' Academy (2018).

In 2012 Jason was granted International Chiropractor of the Year by the Masters Circle.

Jason's professional memberships include:

- British Chiropractic Association
- United Chiropractic Association
- Royal College of Chiropractors (Sports Faculty)

Originally achieving a degree in Pharmacology from Kings College London, Jason soon realised that he found reward not in the medications themselves, but in helping people get better. Jason then went on to graduate from the world-leading Anglo-European College of Chiropractic in 2005.

> "If there's one thing that I love most about the body is that we all have an incredible capacity for healing and repair and that by restoring movement and removing nerve interference through chiropractic, lifestyle advice and specific exercises, in many cases we can provide substantial relief from a number of painful conditions without risking the various side effects associated with taking medications or more invasive procedures.
>
> - Dr Jason Gould

Also by Jason Gould

visit www.5tothrive.co.uk to find out more and order

Printed in Great Britain
by Amazon

36851001R00126